THE BOY

in

THE PICTURE

THE BOY
in
THE PICTURE

The Craigellachie Kid and
the Driving of the Last Spike

RAY ARGYLE

NATURAL HERITAGE BOOKS
A MEMBER OF THE DUNDURN GROUP
TORONTO

Project Editor: Jane Gibson
Editor: Nicole Chaplin
Design: Jesse Hooper
Printer: Marquis

Library and Archives Canada Cataloguing in Publication

Argyle, Ray
      The boy in the picture : the Craigellachie kid and the driving / by Ray Argyle.

Includes bibliographical references and index.
Also issued in electronic format.
ISBN 978-1-55488-787-3

1. Mallandaine, Edward, 1867-1949--Juvenile literature. 2. Railroads--Canada--History--19th century--Juvenile literature. 3. Canadian Pacific Railway Company--History--19th century--Juvenile literature. 4. Railroads--Canada--Employees--Biography--Juvenile literature. 5. Canada--History--1867---Juvenile literature. I. Title.

HE2808.2.M34A74 2010   j385.092   C2010-902402-8

1   2   3   4   5   14   13   12   11   10

We acknowledge the support of the **Canada Council for the Arts** and the **Ontario Arts Council** for our publishing program. We also acknowledge the financial support of the **Government of Canada** through the **Canada Book Fund** and **The Association for the Export of Canadian Books**, and the **Government of Ontario** through the **Ontario Book Publishers Tax Credit program**, and the **Ontario Media Development Corporation**.

Care has been taken to trace the ownership of copyright material used in this book. The author and the publisher welcome any information enabling them to rectify any references or credits in subsequent editions.

                                                                                                    J. Kirk Howard, President

Printed and bound in Canada.
www.dundurn.com

Dundurn Press
3 Church Street, Suite 500
Toronto, Ontario, Canada
M5E 1M2

Gazelle Book Services Limited
White Cross Mills
High Town, Lancaster, England
LA1 4XS

Dundurn Press
2250 Military Road
Tonawanda, NY
U.S.A. 14150

For Christopher, Logan, Sarah, and Jenna

CONTENTS

ACKNOWLEDGEMENTS

When I decided to write Edward Mallandaine's story, I jotted down my recollections of all the tales he'd told me of his youthful adventures. Growing up, we lived in a house he'd built and I looked forward to him coming around every month to collect the rent from my dad. That's when he'd tell me stories of his exploits. When I turned to books about the construction of the Canadian Pacific Railway, I soon realized I would have to go much deeper. Fortunately, I had a lot of help along the way.

The staff of the British Columbia Archives were very helpful in providing me access to their files of Edward's letters and family records. The Glenbow Museum in Calgary offered a treasure trove on Edward's work with the CPR, and I wish to thank their staff, especially Lindsay Moir, for valuable assistance.

Not many small towns have two museums, but that is the case in Revelstoke, British

Columbia. I am especially grateful to Jennifer Dunkerson of the Revelstoke Railway Museum for her assistance and support. She always had time to take telephone calls from myself and my publisher, and was enthusiastic in her endorsement of this project. Cathy English of the Revelstoke Museum and Archives was generous with her time in helping me track down facts about leading personalities from Edward's day

The Creston Museum and Archives in Creston, British Columbia, is the repository of much information about the town's early history and Edward Mallandaine's role in establishing that community. I was greatly assisted by its director, Tammy Hardwick, who scoured through back copies of the Creston *Review* for articles by and about Edward.

This book would not have been possible without the enthusiastic support of Barry Penhale, publisher emeritus of Natural Heritage Books. I am grateful for his encouragement. I also wish to thank Nicole Chaplin, for her meticulous editing of the manuscript.

To my knowledge, Pierre Berton's *The Last Spike: The Great Railway 1881-1885* was the first widely read book to recognize Edward's presence at the ceremony in Craigellachie. I want to express my appreciation to Elsa Franklin, who was Pierre's manager, for her help and encouragement for *The Boy in the Picture.*

I first wrote about Edward Mallandaine for *The Beaver* magazine (now *Canada's History Magazine*). I am indebted to Nelle Oosterom for her award-winning presentation of that article and her ongoing support.

My grateful appreciation goes to my partner Deborah Windsor for her everlasting inspiration, helpfulness, and comfort.

INTRODUCTION

This is the story of Edward Mallandaine, the boy in the picture of the driving of the Last Spike. This photo, perhaps the most famous in Canadian history, marked the completion of the Canadian Pacific Railway (CPR) across Canada. It was taken early on the morning of November 7, 1885, in Craigellachie, British Columbia.

I had the privilege of knowing Edward when he was a very old man and I was a young boy. I have drawn on accounts he left and stories he told me to write this tale of his journey along tote roads and the newly laid tracks of the railway, past "hostess houses" and "Chinese joss houses," into hotels crowded with rough characters, through mountain passes filled with beautiful scenery, and into the lawlessness of remote towns and railway camps.

Today, we enjoy instant communication by phone and the Internet, and think nothing of accessing music, videos, and pictures online. We are only hours away, by plane, from any other place on earth. It may be hard to imagine what it was like when Edward, just eighteen — and looking even younger — set out on his great adventure.

News travelled slowly in Edward's day. The big story during his teenage years was the North-West Rebellion. Edward lived in Victoria, B.C., and the accounts he read in his local newspaper, the *British Colonist*, about the fighting on the prairies were often days old. Right away, he wanted to get in on the action. Accounts from those days tell of how he wanted "to fight the Indians," as First Nations people were known at that time.

Edward probably had little understanding of the true causes of the North-West Rebellion — of how Louis Riel had struggled to obtain justice for his people, the mixed-blood Métis of the plains, and for Natives who had lost their hunting grounds and were being driven into reserves. But with the enthusiasm of youth, he was determined to join the battle.

As it turned out, Edward was too late. The fighting was over by the time he had slogged his way east by boat, train, horseback, and on foot.

Fate had a different destination for Edward. He talked his way into a contract with the Post Office Department to ride a pony between Eagle Pass Landing and the town of Farwell (now Revelstoke), delivering supplies and newspapers to the workers on the railway, and picking up mail and packages. He spent an adventurous summer until the railway was finished, at the beginning of November 1885.

The night before the driving of the Last Spike, Edward clambered aboard a flatcar loaded with steel rails and clung for his life as the train drove through a blinding blizzard to reach Craigellachie. Sleepless and half-frozen, he was determined to put himself in the soon-to-be famous photograph that marks the occasion when Canada was bound together, coast-to-coast, by the transcontinental railway.

The Last Spike was only the first great adventure of Edward's life. He went on to do important work for the CPR and helped found the town of Creston, B.C. He served his community as a magistrate and politician, respected throughout British Columbia. After leading the Kootenay Regiment of the Canadian Army Forestry Corps in the First World War, he became a lieutenant colonel in the Canadian Army Reserve. From that day on, he was known as Colonel Mallandaine, the title by which I knew him.

When Edward died, I was close to the age he had been at Craigellachie: Canada's entire history as a nation has unfolded, from Confederation to the age of terrorism, during the lifetimes of just the two of us. Today's Canada is held together by forces that have long since replaced the railway. It is time to draw again on the legacy of Craigellachie, and the burning ambition that one young man brought to that time and place — to be in the picture, and to be a leading actor in the building of a boisterous, confident country.

I have meshed storytelling with historical record in writing this tribute to Edward Mallandaine. It is dedicated to all young men and women who yearn for adventure. May they be as determined as he was to find it.

Ray Argyle

CHAPTER 1

EDWARD LOOKS FOR TROUBLE

The thing about Edward was, he couldn't stay out of trouble. It was the one thing he was never shy about. At school, he had no difficulty mastering his lessons, but trouble seemed to follow him around. One could never be sure whether trouble found him, or Edward found trouble.

Take the time when his teacher at Victoria Central School, Mr. Pleace, a tall, stern, and fiery-tempered schoolmaster, shouted at him:

"Eddie, you bag of fleas, stop your squirming. You will never set the harbour on fire."

The reason Mr. Pleace shouted at him was that Edward learned his lessons so quickly, he fell easily into boredom. He had to find something else to do — and what he found usually got him into trouble.

This time, Edward was daydreaming about fishing: it was his favourite pastime. He'd sit on a rock on the edge of Victoria Harbour and drop in his line, bearing an enticing hook camouflaged with a cleverly tied imitation bug, or fly. The young salmon and sea trout were often fooled by Edward's flies.

And on his lap, that fateful day, Edward was tying a new fly that he hoped to try out right after school.

When Mr. Pleace told Edward he'd never set the harbour on fire, he took it as a challenge. He decided right then that he'd show the schoolmaster that he could, indeed, set the harbour on fire.

He pondered the conundrum as he meandered along Simcoe Street on his way to his home in Victoria's James Bay district. He wondered if anyone had ever set the sea aflame. He talked it over with his younger brother Frederick, when he got home.

Courtesy B.C. Archives A-06466.

Edward's childhood home on Simcoe Street in Victoria, British Columbia. A C.C. Pemberton photo, 1935.

Together, they decided it could be done. They rummaged around their backyard and found a large, discarded wooden box. After collecting shavings from their woodpile and crumpling up some old copies of the *British Colonist* newspaper, they stuffed the whole mess into the box, and poured oil all over it. Then, the two of them went down to the shore.

"Give me that match, I'll light the paper," Edward told his brother.

Once he was sure it was burning well, he pushed the box out onto the water.

Unfortunately, they'd chosen to launch the fiery carrier just a few feet from the James Bay Bridge, a wooden structure that spanned the Inner Harbour. The tidal current, aided by a brisk breeze, carried the box straight up against the bridge. The burning box soon ignited a piling and in a flash, the bridge was on fire.

A man fishing from a rowboat saved the bridge. He saw the fire and rowed over hurriedly. Using his bailing can, he quickly extinguished the flames.

The boys could hear the man calling to them.

"You kids will be in a pack of trouble if I catch you," he shouted and started rowing quickly to shore.

Edward and Fred ran off, terrified at what they had done but jubilant at having actually set fire to the harbour. That night, all of Victoria was agog at the attempt to burn James Bay Bridge.

As soon as Edward's class assembled the next morning, he shot up his hand, snapping his fingers to gain the attention of the teacher.

"Well, flea bag, what is it you want now?" Mr. Pleace asked. "I suppose you've made up some fantastical excuse for not having done your homework."

"Oh, no Mr. Pleace, it's not about my homework. You said I'd never set the harbour on fire. Well, you're wrong, Mr. Pleace. I *did* set the harbour on fire. Really and truly I did."

If Edward expected praise, he was gravely mistaken.

"You did?" Mr. Pleace exclaimed. "I see you're destructive as well as lazy. We know how to fix a boy like you!"

And with that, he yanked Edward from his seat, grabbed hold of his collar, and dragged him to the front of the room.

"Look at this sorry specimen, children. And let this be a lesson to all of you," he said, pulling out the strap.

In Edward's day, it was common for teachers to beat their pupils when they did something that displeased them.

After, Edward boasted to his friends how it was. "Mr. Pleace gave me one of the best floggings I ever had from him! Still, I can claim to be the only one who ever set Victoria Harbour on fire — and that's something!"

Edward Mallandaine grew up in the very British town of Victoria, British Columbia. During Edward's boyhood, it had already become the biggest town on Vancouver Island. It was also the capital of British Columbia, which had joined Canada as a province based on the promise that it would be connected with the rest of the country by railway.

Victoria was a typical colonial outpost during Edward's school years. The Union Jack flew proudly from the Birdcage, the building that housed the legislative assembly of the young province. The city was built around the magnificent Inner Harbour on the southern tip of Vancouver Island. Edward thought it must have the most beautiful setting of any city in the world.

As a seaport, Victoria attracted a colourful array of characters. There were proper British settlers who brought all their traditions to this new land. Roaming seamen were left wandering the waterfront when their vessels left port without them. Miners en route from California to the gold fields of central British Columbia kept the town's saloons busy. Chinese workers, penniless and adrift, had come to "Gold Mountain" to earn money to support their families back home. They squatted in Chinatown, hoping for the day they could bring their wives and children over.

Edward grew up with his town, as well as with Canada. He was born on June 1, 1867, exactly a month before the Dominion of Canada came into being when the Province of Canada (modern day Quebec and Ontario) joined with the colonies of New Brunswick and Nova Scotia in Confederation. The new nation soon spread west. When British Columbia joined in 1871, Canada was complete from coast to coast.

Edward's teen years were exciting ones. He was a good-looking boy, with sandy-coloured hair and hazel eyes. He did all the things a boy likes to do: he clambered over the rocky shoreline of Victoria Harbour to cast lines for salmon and sea trout; he liked books, and made his father buy all the latest titles, including *The Adventures of Tom Sawyer* by Mark Twain. As Edward devoured every word, he imagined himself in company with the young hero who lived on the Mississippi River. Like Tom, Edward loved the water and had a zest for new experiences.

Edward's experience with people of other races was somewhat limited. With his friends, he sometimes dared to explore the mysterious laneways of Victoria's Chinatown. The boys ran screaming when they encountered a "son of heaven," imagining that the little men in pigtails would harm them if they were caught. In their hearts, Edward and his friends knew they were in no danger.

Edward's position as the oldest of the five Mallandaine children conferred certain privileges on him. He got to stay up later than the others, and was more or less left on his own as to how he spent his time. Whenever he could, whatever he did, he did it with Fred, who was just fourteen months younger. Together, they swam and played cricket for the James Bay Athletic Association. Then there were Edward's two sisters, Louisa and Harriet, and finally the youngest of the lot, Charles.

Edward especially liked playing big brother to Charles. He was eight years his junior, born in 1875. Edward vied with his sisters for the little boy's attention. He could never say no when the lad pleaded to go along with him and Fred on one of their more harmless adventures.

Edward must have got his sense of adventure from his parents. Both had dared to take on unknown risks in search of excitement.

His father, also named Edward, had travelled the world by the time he arrived in Victoria in 1858. He was a descendant of a Protestant Huguenot family from France. In the seventeenth century they fled their homeland with other Protestants to escape religious persecution. The Huguenots had faced the same kind of discrimination that other minorities, like the Jews throughout Europe, Blacks in North and South America, and the aboriginals of Canada and Australia, have also suffered.

The Mallandaines landed in London, England's East End, where they fell into the busy life of the city's guild of master silk weavers. Edward's grandfather, John West Mallandaine, worked his way up in the British East India Company and became the British military commander in Singapore. That was where Edward's father was born.

After the family moved back to England, Edward's father tried his hand at gold mining in Australia. When that didn't work out, he returned to London where he worked as an apprentice to an architect. He learned enough to set himself up as an architect and marry. Unfortunately, his wife died eight days after giving birth to a daughter and the little girl died before her first birthday. Heartbroken, he sold his home and possessions, and borrowed seventy pounds from his sister. That gave him the money to start life afresh in Victoria, in the colony of Vancouver Island.

Edward's father prospered in Victoria. He worked for a while as a teacher in a private school, then bought the school and started the city's first night school for adults. Next he struck on a brilliant idea. The city was growing but its newcomers were strangers to their neighbours, so he decided to publish a directory listing the names and addresses of everyone in Victoria. People paid to put notices advertising their businesses in this, the first city directory in British North America.

Later, he worked as an architect and designed buildings in Victoria and New Westminster, and in Portland and San Francisco in the United States as well. He loved to play the organ and paint pictures. In fact, many of his paintings are still held in the British Columbia Archives in Victoria.

Edward's mother, Louisa Townsend, also led an adventurous life. Feeling she had no prospects in England, she boarded the S.S. *Tynemouth* to come to Victoria. It was a bride ship, so-called because it was filled with respectable young women who had agreed to go to Vancouver Island where there was a shortage of marriageable girls. She had a storm-tossed

The mighty Thompson River surges into the Fraser River, in a scene painted in 1877 by Edward Mallandaine Sr.

trip around Cape Horn at the tip of South America before landing in Victoria. She met Edward's father when they both sang in the choir at St. John's Anglican Church.

When Edward was fourteen, in 1881, he completed the last of the classes offered at Victoria Central School; it was typical in those days for boys and girls to finish school at that age.

By then, Edward's father had branched out to become a surveyor and had landed a contract with the Canadian Pacific Railway. He was given the assignment of surveying the route for the new line from Port Moody on Burrard Inlet, up the Fraser River as far as Yale. He took Edward along with him, thinking he would be able to get him a job at a salmon cannery in New Westminster.

But the cannery owner had other ideas.

"We're only hiring Chinese workers," the owner said. "They're reliable and they'll work for less than Whites."

This attitude upset Edward. He didn't think it was fair. When his father arranged for him to work in the survey party, though, he soon forgot about the cannery. He learned to sight land levels through the survey equipment and marvelled at the beautiful mountains that rose majestically beyond the Fraser River.

I'd like to follow the railway through those mountains someday, he thought.

The end of summer brought a close to the survey job and Edward returned with his father to Victoria. He'd always been skilled with his hands, and he soon found a job as a carpenter, helping to build houses and new stores. He learned architecture from his father. That winter, he went as far away as Portland, in the United States, to work construction jobs.

Edward was at home in the spring of 1885 when he read about the trouble on the Canadian Prairies in the *British Colonist*, the newspaper everybody in Victoria relied on for news of the world. He knew right away that he wanted to get in on the action.

Edward, like any other seventeen-year-old, was excited with the news that Louis Riel, the leader of the Plains Métis, was back in Canada from exile in Montana. He would likely stir up the Natives and start another rebellion.

Courtesy B.C. Archives HP004383.

"PRESIDENT" LOUIS RIEL.

Métis leader Louis Riel's hanging in 1885 aroused bitter feelings between French-speaking Canadians, especially in Quebec, and people in English Canada who applauded his execution.

From Traitor to Hero

Louis Riel, hanged as a traitor, is now seen as one of the builders of Canada. The architect of the North-West Rebellion of 1885 and an earlier rebellion that led to the formation of the province of Manitoba, where his memory is honoured every February on Riel Day.

Louis Riel was a fiery man, and many considered him a little crazy. He was deeply religious and had fled to the United States following the troubles in Manitoba. Three times the Métis people elected him as their Member of Parliament, but he was never able to take his seat at Ottawa.

Riel travelled to the Saskatchewan Prairie in 1884 in response to a plea from his friend and local Métis leader, Gabriel Dumont. The Métis had settled on land that the government hadn't yet surveyed. They were later told they would have to pay two dollars an acre — an enormous sum at that time, which none of them could afford.

His return to Canada set off alarms at the Hudson's Bay Company trading posts and forts manned by the North-West Mounted Police. But not everyone expected trouble. Father André, a Catholic missionary, wrote to the governor of the North-West Territories, Edgar Dewdney, to say that Riel "has acted and spoken in a quiet and sensible way." The government resisted advice by the North-West Mounted Police officer closest to the scene, Inspector Leif Crozier, to come to terms with the Métis.

Riel set up a Provisional Government of Saskatchewan and proclaimed a Revolutionary Bill of Rights. He chose Batoche, on the South Saskatchewan River, as his capital. When Riel and Dumont heard that the Mounties were about to arrest them, they ransacked local stores, and seized weapons and supplies. In a pitched battle at Duck Lake, a dozen Mounties and five Métis were killed. The Plains Cree, with the reluctant approval of their chief Big Bear, joined the fight.

Other battles followed, but a superior force of Canadian Militia, shipped out from Ontario on the newly built Canadian Pacific Railway, aided by the North-West Mounted Police under the command of Colonel Sam Steele, soon put down the rebellion. Riel surrendered. He was hanged in Regina on November 16, 1885.

"I'd like to go and fight the Indians," Edward told his father. "They're rising up against the Queen. I want to help stop them."

The idea of joining soldiers on the Prairies filled Edward's head day and night. He'd read about a family taken prisoner by the chief of the Plains Cree, Big Bear. He could just see himself marching with the troops under a vast prairie sky. At night, he dreamt of rescuing a helpless girl from Big Bear's clutches.

Courtesy Library and Archives Canada C-002425 [1].

Edward's ambition was to fight in the North-West Rebellion. This painting by Fred Curzon (1862–90) depicts the Battle of Fish Creek.

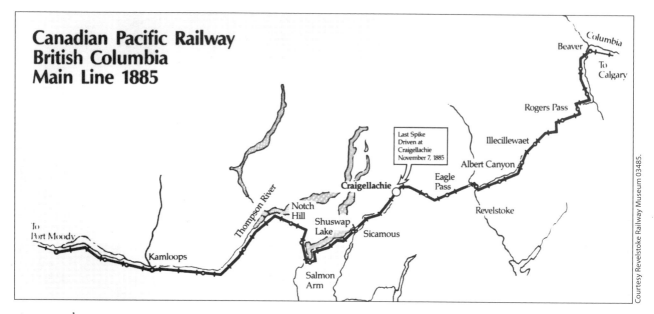

The Last Spike map: a blueprint of the main line, pinpointing Craigellachie, where rail crews from east and west linked up to complete the Canadian Pacific Railway.

Edward, along with other Canadians, might have thought differently had he better understood what was happening to the First Nations in the North-West Territories.

Every day, Edward scanned the *British Colonist* and pressed his father for permission to light out for the Prairies. There was news of more battles, and most of it wasn't good. Then came a turn for the better: a force of three thousand Canadian Militia men had been rushed from Ontario to the Prairies. They travelled quickly over the newly built Canadian Pacific Railway line.

Even during the fighting, railway workers, called "navvies," were laying track through the Rocky Mountains. Other workers were pushing east from the Pacific Coast, following the route surveyed by Edward's father. It wouldn't be long before they joined up somewhere in the mountains. When that happened, Canada would finally have a railway running from coast to coast.

"You've got to let me go," Edward told his parents. "Else I'll run away. You can't stop me. I hate this place!" Edward was getting angry. He was fed up with being told what to do.

"If you leave now, don't bother coming home again," Edward's father said. "You're learning to be an architect. I won't have you going off to some God forsaken part of the country that you know nothing about."

Edward suddenly saw his chance.

"What about when you lit out for Australia? I suppose you knew what you were getting into."

Edward saw a smile come to his mother's face.

"You know he's right," she said to his father. "But he looks so young for his age. I hope people won't think he's a runaway."

"Well, the army seems to have things under control," his father answered. "Maybe we could consider letting Edward go. I'm sure he'll be well looked after by the soldiers. But he's got to promise to come back and finish up his apprenticeship. I want him to be an architect."

"Oh, I will, I will," Edward answered happily.

Finally, perhaps in recognition of Edward's eighteenth birthday, his parents gave in at last.

"I'm going, I'm going!" Edward shouted as he bounced onto the porch of his friend Jimmy's house. He babbled excitedly. Jimmy listened, his mouth hanging open. He couldn't understand why Edward would want to travel to the North-West when there was lots of fun to be had right here in Victoria.

"I guess we won't be going fishing on Saturday then," Jimmy said. Edward dashed off without answering. He had to pack up the stuff he'd need for the trip.

Edward got his father to buy him a ticket on the steamer to New Westminster. From there, he'd ride a Canadian Pacific train as far upcountry as it would take him. He'd have to make his way through the mountains on foot or by horseback. Then he'd be on his way again by train. He just knew the militia would be glad to see him.

Why, they'll probably give me a uniform and a gun on my very first day. Reporting for duty, Sir! There's a war to be won!

CHAPTER 2

CAUGHT
IN THE FLAMES

A cooling breeze brushed Edward's face as he walked up the gangplank of the S.S. *Rainbow* just after eight o'clock one Sunday evening. The whole family had attended morning services at St. John's Anglican Church. Edward's father told the minister that he was leaving on the evening steamer for the North-West.

"I'll say a special prayer for Edward's safety," Reverend Wilson told the family. "May God look after him."

Edward turned for one more look at his family gathered on the dock below. They were waving to him. All had smiles except his mother, who wiped a tear with her handkerchief, then looked quickly away. The steamer would be leaving in a few minutes for New Westminster. For the hundredth time, Edward checked his ticket and saw again that he was assigned to cabin C-3. This meant he'd make the voyage across the Strait of Georgia on the ship's lower deck.

Edward went straight to his cabin, stowed his satchel, and returned to the second deck to watch the departure from Victoria Harbour. As the *Rainbow* slid away from the dock Edward ran his eyes along the familiar rocky shoreline. *At last I'm on my way*, he thought. *I'll not be back for awhile.* The prospect of adventure sent a tingle down his spine.

Edward knew that the *Rainbow* was owned by the Hudson's Bay Company, but he paid that fact little mind. The steamer was one of several built in England that were used to ferry supplies in and out of various towns and trading posts up and down the British Columbia coast. Plumes of grey and black smoke billowed from its single smokestack, evidence that the ship's wood-burning furnace was now filled with blazing logs. Close to the prow of the *Rainbow* stood the pilot house, and behind the smokestack were the top deck cabins, reserved for first-class passengers. They would enjoy fine views through their portholes, even if the breeze wafted the occasional spark or bits of ash their way.

Once on open water, the *Rainbow* began to rock with the swell caused by the waters of the Pacific flowing into the narrow gaps of the Strait of Georgia, the span of water separating Vancouver Island from the Mainland. It was getting dark and Edward could just pick out the blurred shapes of the San Juan Islands off of starboard.

The islands were now American territory. Edward remembered what he'd learned in school about the Pig War. In 1859, an American settler on the islands had killed a Hudson's Bay Company pig. Soon, American troops were facing off against British soldiers intent on arresting the farmer. It took the German Kaiser, Wilhelm I, to settle the dispute. He had awarded the islands to the United States.

Edward preferred to cast his eyes in the other direction, toward the Gulf Islands on his portside. No one challenged their belonging to Canada. He could just make out the Pender Islands, and beyond them, Saturna Island. He'd heard it had especially beautiful beaches.

As he stood at the ship's rail, a man in a bowler hat approached him.

"Well, young man, where are you bound?" Edward told the man, who said his name was Duncan Ferguson, that he was going to enlist in the Canadian Militia, somewhere on the Prairies.

"Aye, m'lad, I think that fight's about done," Mr. Ferguson said.

He went on to tell Edward how a force of troops and North-West Mounted Police were battling the rebels. Mr. Ferguson spoke with such a thick Scottish brogue that Edward couldn't understand all he was saying.

"In all my thirty years in this country I've never ken such confabulation."

Edward said he was going anyway.

"You never know when the Indians might rise up and attack White settlers."

The *Rainbow* was at full speed now, making between ten and twelve knots. That meant it would take nine or ten hours to complete the hundred kilometre journey to New Westminster. Edward thought he may as well go to bed; he wanted to be up early. His ticket included breakfast, and he looked forward to being awake when they entered the estuary of the Fraser River.

The next morning, with an appetite amplified by the bracing sea air, Edward was among the first to line up outside the dining room. Looking out, he could make out a long stretch of flat, empty land reaching back from the river, and beyond that, the sudden rise of mountains. There was a lumber mill and, next to it, a cannery where a lot of people were moving salmon onto long tables.

The dining room doors were flung open and Edward wasn't ready for the rush of passengers. He felt himself being carried through the doors, and was pushed aside as men scrambled to take seats at the tables. Somebody knocked a Black waiter off his feet and the large platter of eggs he was carrying clattered to the floor. By the time Edward found a seat and waited for food to come his way, there was little left. He filled up on buns, toast, and coffee.

When the *Rainbow* docked in New Westminster, Edward saw that, since his last visit, the town had spread out further along the river's north shore. About fifteen hundred people lived there, but it was still only about a quarter of the size of Victoria. A few three- and four-storey stone-and-brick buildings hugged the waterfront. Beyond them, on a hill sloping

Courtesy B.C. Archives A-01594.

New Westminster in Edward's day, viewed here in a photograph taken from the Fraser River, was a rowdy river town.

up toward the forest, wooden houses were scattered as though they'd been dropped by some strong wind that had blown through the place. On the other side of the river there was nothing but mud flats.

The usual commotion met the ship's arrival. Dock workers started unloading cargo and passengers streamed off, one by one. After disembarking, Edward went straight to the Royal George hotel, where he and his father had once stayed. There was a new man at the front desk. At first, he didn't want to give Edward a room.

Rascals and Rowdies in a Royal City

New Westminster was a rough and ready river port, filled with rascals and rowdies. Queen Victoria named it after the city of Westminster, which is the area of London where the parliament buildings for the United Kingdom are located. Because of this connection, New Westminster became known as the Royal City.

New Westminster is the oldest city in western Canada and was the first capital of British Columbia. It lost the capital to Victoria when the colonies of British Columbia and Vancouver Island were united in 1866.

Thousands of miners passed through New Westminster in the Gold Rush, and it became the main outfitting point for prospectors. Known to the Chinese as Saltwater City, it had a large Chinatown along Front Street, one of the city's most important streets. As the land became more valuable, the Chinese were pushed out to an area known as "the Swamp." Today, New Westminster is a prosperous and beautiful city of more than 60,000 people.

"What are you doing here alone, kid?" he demanded. Edward told him he was going by boat to Yale and then by train up the Fraser Canyon.

"In that case, you'll be here two nights," he told Edward. "The next boat's on Wednesday. That'll be fifty cents a night."

Edward dug a dollar in coins out of his change purse, signed the register, and went to his room. The window looked out over the river and he could see goods being loaded on a steamer tied up at the dock. It was the *Adelaide*, the little vessel that would take him up the Fraser River to Yale. That was as far as boats could go before reaching the impassable rapids in the Fraser Canyon: no boat could navigate such a treacherous stretch. Rails had been laid north of Yale, as far as Van Horne (also known as Savona), a small settlement named after William Van Horne, the general manager of the railway.

Edward spent the next morning wandering up and down New Westminster's two streets of stores and warehouses. Bored, he bought bread and cheese and climbed the hill behind the town where he sat among the trees and looked down on the broad Fraser River. It was six-hundred metres wide and Edward could make out small fishing boats, which he guessed were trolling for salmon. Closer to shore, tugs pulled logs bound for the sawmill. On the other side of the river, flatlands stretched away to the south. He could see the peak of a large mountain in the distance. His father had told him that it was Mount Baker, and that it was just across the line in the United States.

Edward was up early on Wednesday morning, excited to be setting out on the next leg of his journey. The *Adelaide* had been designed specially to navigate the tricky waters of the Fraser and rode smoothly up the wide river.

Edward saw flocks of ducks and geese feeding in the shallow waters where the river had overflowed onto the surrounding flatland. That evening, the *Adelaide* docked at a small camp set amid steep mountains that ran right down to the water's edge; they were a magnificent sight. Everything seemed to be narrowing at this spot, as if the river was being pushed into a crevice between the mountains.

The river was running faster than when Edward had been there with his father, and the *Adelaide* moved more slowly as it pushed against the downward current. It almost stalled a few times, and once it even spun around before the captain could order more fuel for the furnace. Then Edward heard three sharp blasts of the *Adelaide's* whistle: the captain came out of the pilot house and told the passengers he could take them no further.

"The current's running too strong," he shouted across the deck. "We've had high water all this year, too much snow in the mountains. Still melting. I'll have to let you all off at Emery Bar. Just around the bend. You've five miles to go to Yale. You'll have to walk it, unless you take the stagecoach."

There were twenty passengers on the boat and most grumbled as they disembarked. Edward noticed that Mr. Ferguson was among the passengers going ashore. It didn't take long for Edward to realize that Emery Bar was nothing more than a stagecoach stop close to the opening of the Fraser Canyon. He saw Chinese workers hanging around the dock. A livery stable had a sign, CARRIAGES FOR RENT. Some of the passengers headed for the stable, but Edward knew he'd have to walk. He put his cloth hat on his head, flung his satchel over his back, and set out on the narrow, rutted road that ran along the river bank.

As Edward walked along, Mr. Ferguson caught up to him, a little out of breath from having hurried to join him.

"It might be a good idea to stick together." Edward didn't mind, but he wondered if perhaps Mr. Ferguson was afraid of getting lost.

After they'd walked about a mile, following the path high above the Fraser River, the air grew hazy. It wasn't long before Edward smelled something burning. Mr. Ferguson guessed that it must be a forest fire.

"It won't bother us, we're right on the river," he told Edward. "Can always jump in if we have to."

But the smell of burning grew stronger as they walked. Bits of ash rained down on their heads. Edward knocked a spark off his shoulder. Then, as they came around a sharp bend, he could see trees on both sides of the trail bursting into flame. The fire was burning its way toward them, as if it was thirsty and trying to reach the river.

"Keep yer head!" Mr. Ferguson shouted. "Follow me! Stay here and we'll be burned up. Better be a coward than a corpse!"

He turned and started running back down the trail.

Edward wasn't sure what to do. The fire seemed to be getting closer but he didn't want to go all the way back to where they'd landed. There was nothing there. Up ahead lay Yale and a train to take him east.

Maybe I can jump into the river if I need to, Edward thought. *I'm not turning back*.

The forest was ablaze above him. The firestorm came in great sheets of flames and the sky filled with clouds of smoke. It had been a dry summer in the mountains, and the pine and spruce needles, filled with resin, burned and crackled like firecrackers. The noise of the fire was almost as terrifying as the heat of the flames.

Edward had heard that people who breathed forest fire air could die on the spot, their lungs burned to a crisp. He imagined himself as a bundle of burned bones on the forest floor and shuddered.

Before Edward knew it, his hat was on fire. He felt the heat on his head and smelled his hair burning. He slapped at his hat, threw it off, and ran his hands through his hair. Pieces of singed hair came loose from his scalp! Breaking into a run, Edward left the road and made his way down a steep bank to the river's edge.

He was on the edge of a small clearing, out of the main fire zone. The clearing acted as a natural fire break, confining the blaze. Edward knelt at the river bank and dunked his head in the water. It stung where the cold water touched the burn on his scalp.

"You're a lucky lad," he heard a voice behind him. It was Mr. Ferguson.

"I've come back after ye," he said. "Couldn't leave ye here all alone. Ye didn't see that tree fall almost on ye. It came down just behind ye. I had to jump over it to get clear. We could 'ave been burned to a crisp!"

CHAPTER 3

A DARK NIGHT AT EAGLE LANDING

It took Edward and Mr. Ferguson an hour to walk to Yale. There was no sign of the fire near the town. A train, its engine puffing white smoke, shunted up and down the tracks. It was collecting cars and depositing others on spurs that ran off the main track. When it pulled up in front of a water tower, a man lowered a long trough and let water pour into the engine's boilers. It would take a full tank to make enough steam to pull the train up the steady incline of the canyon and into the high country beyond.

The train was just getting ready to leave as Edward collected his ticket from the station master. It had two coaches, as well as several freight cars and a tender loaded with wood for the boiler. The coaches were crude affairs, just rough lumber painted a dull red. Inside, people sat on benches that ran down either side. There were spaces for windows, but they had no glass. Edward took a seat near the door and stuffed his satchel between his legs; Mr. Ferguson sat opposite him.

Courtesy B.C. Archives PDP04426.

Building a railway through the Fraser Canyon took sweat, guts, and dynamite, and led to many injuries and deaths especially among Chinese workers.

Courtesy Revelstoke Railway Museum c74968.

Tunnel No. 7 above Yale allowed trains to cling to Fraser Canyon cliffs.

As the train clattered off into the canyon, the coaches rattled and swayed: the rails had only just been laid. They hadn't yet settled into the road bed, but Edward was too busy looking out at a wilderness of rocks and staggering peaks to be bothered by the rough ride. Mr. Ferguson was chattering to the other passengers in his Scottish brogue, telling them about the fire he and Edward had escaped.

"I'm a Highlander, by the grace of God," Edward heard him say, "but ah dinnae ken a fire like the one we was just through. That's a brave lad, young Eddie, he found the way down to the river. That's what saved us."

As the train chugged along, Edward saw that the wall of the canyon stretched almost straight down below the tracks. He could see water, muddy with silt, churning and frothing a hundred feet below. The train was occasionally plunged into darkness as it passed through tunnels, which had been dug out where the mountainside was almost vertical.

After a few hours, the canyon widened and, before Edward knew it, the train had left the narrow Fraser River and begun to make its way along another, quieter stream. He knew from its clear, green water that they had entered the valley of the South Thompson River, named after the great explorer who had first travelled through the Rocky Mountains and into British Columbia.

That evening, the train stopped at Van Horne, close to where the river widened out into Kamloops Lake. Van Horne was more of a construction camp than a village and piles of steel rails lay beside the tracks. Gangs of men drove oxen that were dragging timber, which would be made into ties on which the rails would be set. Off in the distance, he could see a collection of tents.

Courtesy Revelstoke Railway Museum c75088.

Chinese workers were involved in clearing routes through the mountains on the great railway project. They lived in makeshift shacks, such as these, along the way.

A line of men moved back and forth between the railway and the tents. Edward noticed that shacks were scattered alongside the railway, which all seemed to be filled with Chinese workers. Outside one shack there was a man sitting on a chair getting his hair cut. The barber was careful not to touch his pigtail, which Edward had heard was their way of showing loyalty to the Chinese emperor.

The men wore loose clothes that looked like pajamas. Some had only sandals on their feet and most were wearing flat, wide-brimmed hats. The men belonged to the construction gangs collected by the railway contractor, Andrew Onderdonk. He'd come up from the States, where he helped build the Northern Pacific Railway. His task was to oversee the final completion of the Canadian Pacific.

Edward knew that a lot of people didn't like the idea of the railway bringing in workers from China. But he'd also heard that this was the only to get the railway built on time. He'd read in the *British Colonist* that the prime minister, Sir John A. Macdonald, had made that clear to Parliament, when he said that if they wanted the railway they'd have to accept the use of Chinese labour. "[E]ither you must have [Chinese] labour or you cannot have a railway." Edward had heard there were six thousand Chinese men working on the railway; it seemed like they were all there in Van Horne.

The countryside was flatter there, and drier and browner. Track was being laid more quickly, but still there was no train service east of this camp. Edward had to wait two days for the next steamer, which would take passengers through a series of lakes, beginning with Kamloops Lake and ending on the eastern-most shore of Shuswap Lake.

The steamer that Edward boarded on Saturday was even smaller than the *Adelaide*. Captain Fortune stood at the narrow gangplank leading onto the *Peerless* and collected tickets. He noticed Edward was travelling alone. "Where are you bound for, son?"

By now, Edward was a little fed up with all the questions people kept asking him. Some seemed to think he was just a child who shouldn't be going about on his own.

"I'm going east," Edward answered, showing Captain Fortune his ticket.

6,000 Chinese Workers Called Him "Boss"

Andrew Onderdonk was an American railway contractor, born in New York to an old English-Dutch family. He worked on railways in the United States before winning the contract to build the 342-kilometre section of the CPR from Burrard Inlet to Savona, near Kamloops. When he finished that section, he was told to push on and got as far as Eagle Pass, another 202 kilometres, before running out of rails. His crew was left at Craigellachie, where they met the navvies coming from the East. The Last Spike was driven there on November 7, 1885.

As the construction boss for the toughest part of the Canadian Pacific Railway, Onderdonk could never have finished the job without the tireless work of the 6,000 Chinese labourers he brought in from California and China. The Canadian government had insisted that Onderdonk hire Chinese workers because they would work for lower wages than White Canadians. At first, he brought in Chinese workers from California, but most deserted to work in the gold fields. Onderdonk then turned to China where he engaged agents to recruit peasants in an area plagued by famine. Floods and drought had uprooted millions of destitute peasants in Guangdong Province. Those who could find work earned about seven cents a day. They were desperate.

Onderdonk moved his wife and daughter Eva to Yale, British Columbia, for the duration of the project. After completing his work on the CPR, he built a railway in South America and worked on major engineering projects, including the Trent Canal in Ontario and the building of the Victoria Bridge in Montreal. He died in 1905 in New York.

Courtesy Revelstoke Railway Museum 056410 and 070833.

Andrew Onderdonk's wife and his daughter Eva (right) lived in Yale on the Fraser River during construction of the railway.

Edward boarded the *Peerless*, a small paddlewheel vessel, to cross Shuswap Lake.

The village of Kamloops was a key supply point for railway builders, seen here in this photograph from the 1880s.

"Well, that's the way this boat's going, lad. Welcome aboard."

Edward marvelled again at the beauty of the countryside. Rolling hills stretched out from either bank. When they entered Kamloops Lake, he stood at the stern watching as the *Peerless* left behind a frothy wake. He saw Natives for the first time, when the boat stopped at Kamloops; he thought they looked a dismal lot. One was leading a mule up the road from the dock. He was moving slowly and Edward wondered where he was going. Several children played in the dust beside the dock. He was watching them when he noticed Mr. Ferguson standing beside him.

"This is where I get off," he told Edward. "See the smoke from that sawmill up yonder? That's where I make ties for the railway. Got the contract for this whole section of the line."

Mr. Ferguson told Edward that he and Donald A. Smith, the president of the CPR, were boyhood chums from back home in Scotland.

"Aye, we were inseparable in the auld country. And in thirty years in Canada, we've ne'er lost our friendship!"

That night, while Edward slept on board, the steamer navigated its way through the lakes. On Sunday evening, exactly a week after Edward had left home, the *Peerless* tied up at a ramshackle, rough-hewn wooden dock at Eagle Landing. It was dark as the *Peerless* dropped anchor. Edward was afraid: he was stepping into the unknown as he made his way down the gangplank. He could see a number of buildings dimly lit by lanterns shining faintly through their grimy windows and he heard what sounded like celebrating. He was anxious to get to the Prairies where the war was being fought. He wanted to be in it more than ever.

A gang of men stood on the dock watching the passengers alight. They wore rough clothing and most had unkempt beards. Their appearance worried him and he found their language coarse. Several of the men were holding tin cans with candles in them, casting a ghostly air about the place. All together, the sight made him even more nervous.

Suddenly, he heard someone call his name. "Edward! Over here!" He peered through the darkness. Sure enough, he recognized Tom Freeman, a schoolmate who had been two years ahead of him at Victoria Central. Edward was relieved to meet someone he knew.

Courtesy B.C. Archives 8-0324.

A makeshift dock awaited the *Peerless* upon Edward's arrival at Eagle Landing on the east shore of Shuswap Lake. The settlement is now called Sicamous, B.C.

They talked a bit, each explaining what they were up to. Tom said track was being laid eastward from Eagle Landing through Eagle Pass.

"It won't be too many more months before the railway is finished," Tom told him. "Meanwhile, you'll have to beat your way over to Farwell, on the other side of Eagle Pass. The track from the east will be there soon."

Tom offered to show Edward the way to the Royal Hotel. The two set out on a rutted road lined with small buildings. Edward was left standing alone outside the hotel after Tom explained he had to go off a mile or two, to a camp outside the town.

Edward talked to himself a bit while he screwed up enough courage to go inside. He was beginning to realize that being raised in a comfortable home in Victoria hadn't really prepared him for this adventure.

He timidly opened the big wooden door, hewn from cedar slabs from the nearby forest, and entered the Royal Hotel: the place didn't look very royal. He found himself in a long room with a bar running from end to end. Behind it, several men poured drinks for fifty or sixty terribly coarse and rough looking customers, all of whom seemed to be talking at once. Most were swearing, and it seemed to Edward that several were on the verge of fighting.

No one paid Edward any mind. After a minute or two, having become accustomed to the candle light, he convinced himself that no one was likely to hurt him. He approached the bar, where a man who seemed to be in charge stood moving bottles and glasses around. He had a large cigar in his mouth and wore a dirty white apron that hung over a sagging stomach. Edward asked if he could get a room.

The man looked at him quizzically.

"Boy, what are you doing here? We don't get many kids hanging around here on their own."

"I'm on my way to the Rebellion and I'm joining the militia," Edward replied. "But first I need to get to Farwell."

The noise behind Edward seemed to fade away. The seconds slipped by. He heard a tin mug clatter onto the floor. It was as if books were falling, one at a time, off the shelf in his bedroom. He felt a breath on his neck, but was afraid to turn around. Edward looked into the eyes of the man behind the bar, but the man just stared back.

The bartender wiped his mouth with his sleeve. Stray hairs from his nearly bald head fell onto his forehead. While swirling a dirty rag across the counter to soak up a puddle of spilled beer, he began firing questions at Edward.

"How did you get here? What are you going to do at Farwell? Where's your folks?"

Edward decided he'd better give good answers. He spoke truthfully, explaining his wish to join the Canadian Militia, and that he was making his way to Farwell in order to catch a train that would take him onto the Prairies. The bartender mulled over his story.

Finally, the man leaned across the bar, his head only a few inches from Edward's face. "You can have a bed upstairs. It won't cost you anything."

Edward heaved a sigh of relief. Maybe Eagle Landing wasn't going to be so bad after all!

The bartender pointed to a ladder propped against the wall at the end of the bar room. It reminded Edward of the ladders he'd seen in hay barns. *No stairs?*

"That's the way up," the bartender called after him. "You'll find a bed up there."

Edward was weary by now. He pulled himself up the ladder and climbed through the hole in the ceiling. He found himself in a loft lit by a single candle. He could make out rows of folding canvas cots jammed up against either wall. They had thin straw mattresses but no blankets. Not a single one was occupied. He looked around for a toilet, but he couldn't find anything. Through a crack in the floor, he could see into the bar room below. Tobacco smoke drifted up like a fog.

Edward thought about looking elsewhere to sleep, but he was tired. Rather than venture back down the ladder, he chose a cot that stood in the far corner of the loft, its head and one side protected by the walls. He decided to sleep in his clothes. Extracting a small blanket from his satchel, he lay down, put the little bag under his head for a pillow, and tried to fall asleep.

But he couldn't get to sleep. After awhile, he could hear and feel men coming up the ladder. The lone candle had burned out and it was dark, except for the chain of light coming from the crack in the floor. Once in the loft, the men stumbled about, swearing at each other before falling onto the cots in drunken stupors.

A man dropped onto the cot next to Edward. He could sense the heat and the smell of the man's body, as well as his drunken breath. Edward was trembling, wishing he had gone somewhere else. Eventually the men quieted down and Edward managed to fall into a fitful sleep. He woke up often, disturbed by the loud snores coming from the cot next to him.

CHAPTER 4

THUNDER IN THE PASS

It was barely dawn when Edward awoke to the first light of day. He looked around and realized the kind of place he had fallen into: the Royal Hotel was nothing more than a room for men to sleep off their drunkenness. Bodies were sprawled across the cots and on the floor. On the cot next to him, Edward saw a huge Black man lying with his mouth wide open. He rose quietly, picked up his satchel and blanket, and tiptoed between the rows of beds. He had to get away from this room of evil-looking men, and the smell of stale tobacco and whisky.

Edward's first thought was to head down to the dock and take the steamer back to Van Horne. He was tempted to give up on his big idea of joining the militia. At that moment, he wanted nothing more than to be at home. But the dock was bare; the *Peerless* had sailed during the night.

Edward was miserable. His first night at Eagle Landing had sickened him: he wasn't accustomed to this kind of rough life. Then he started to itch and remembered someone on the boat saying that everyone in Eagle Landing was lousy. He didn't know exactly what that meant, or what to do about it. But he thought the water might help.

Since it was a warm July morning, Edward decided to go for a swim. He took off his clothes behind a tree and waded into the lake. The water felt wonderful! When he got out and dressed, he washed his blanket, hoping to remove any trace of whatever might have gotten on it during the night. He was feeling better, so he decided to walk back to the main part of town to try to find some breakfast.

People were beginning to move about the rutted street that ran half a mile along the lakeshore. As he walked along, Edward noticed something strange: there seemed to be hundreds, perhaps thousands, of playing cards scattered in the dirt along the side of the road. He bent down and gathered a handful of them. He picked up an ace of clubs, a king of hearts, and a jack of diamonds. He wondered why all these cards, which seemed to be perfectly good other than being a bit weather-beaten, had been thrown out.

A few men were loitering around the J. Fred Hume and Company dry goods store. Edward decided to ask about the cards lying in the street. He got a quick explanation.

"That's how we keep the gamblers honest," a man with a great bushy beard told him. "A fresh deck of cards for every round of poker. Only use it once. Then throw it out the window. We don't want anybody stacking the deck."

There was a small frame building with a sign hanging in front that said EATS — CHINESE AND CANADIAN near the store. He went in. A Chinese man was standing over a stove cooking for the three customers who were already there. Edward took a seat at the counter and asked for breakfast. The cook gave him a slice of salt pork, a chunk of bread, and tea in a tin mug. The whole meal cost a dollar. *At this rate*, Edward thought, *my money won't last very long*.

After breakfast, Edward explored the side alleys that ran off the main street. It was clear to him that Eagle Landing was one of those places that spring up like a mushroom, and sometimes die in just a few days, like the gold mining towns he'd heard about. He thought everyone must be eager to make money at the expense of the workers, selling them whisky, getting them to gamble, and over-charging for everything. He wondered how long the town would last after the railway was finished and there was no call for the lake steamers to stop there.

Eagle Landing seemed to be made up of one makeshift wooden building after another. There were some general stores, a post office, and a stable that ran a stagecoach service the eighty kilometres over the Monashee Mountains to Farwell. Edward inquired about the cost of a ticket to Farwell.

"It'll cost you twenty-five dollars, that's if there's a seat open on the next stage," the man in the office told him.

Edward was shocked. "That's too much for me, I'll have to walk it." But he didn't like the idea of striking out by himself on a lonely road through the wilderness. He'd been told there were mountain lions and bears in these parts. He decided to walk around some more while he contemplated his prospects.

While Edward was mulling over the mess he'd found himself in he encountered a young man a little older than himself, who was leading two horses. Edward decided to strike up a conversation.

"What are you doing with those horses?" Edward asked.

"They're pack animals, can't you see the stuff they're carrying?" the stranger answered. He went on to explain that he used them when someone wanted stuff taken to the railway camps.

Edward introduced himself; the stranger said his name was Jim Gillett. He seemed friendly. Edward thought it would be good to travel with someone who knew the country, and explained his predicament.

"No point in your hanging around here," Jim told Edward. "You can ride along on one of my horses if you want to go to Farwell. Get yourself some grub down at the general store and meet me in front of the stagecoach office in an hour."

At the general store, Edward chose a pound of ham, a dozen potatoes, and a few ounces of coffee. Then he decided to add three eggs he'd seen sitting on the counter. The storekeeper charged him three dollars and twenty-five cents. *Good thing I don't have to pay for water*, Edward thought, but kept it to himself.

By the time Edward met Jim, it was the hottest part of the day. It took Edward, who had never been on a horse, a couple of tries, but with help he was soon astride his new friend's white mare. They had ridden only a little way before Jim suggested they have another look at the lake. Edward didn't mind, but he found it almost as hard to get off the horse as to get

Courtesy Revelstoke Railway Museum 02386.

Reliable pack horses were essential. Without them, the surveyors would have faced an impossible job.

on it! The horses grazed on grass while the two young men lay on their backs and talked about their hopes for the future.

"I'm gonna get me a farm," Jim told Edward. "Then I won't have to wander all through this God-forsaken country tryin' to find a square meal."

Edward said the idea of farming didn't much interest him. He was still intent on joining the militia.

It was at this point that Jim produced a bobble of twine and two fish hooks, which he attached to the string, placing them about a foot apart. He waded into the lake, threw out the line as far as he could, and waited for the fish to bite. A half hour later, he had four nice trout. At five o'clock, they made a little fire and cooked the fish. Edward decided he'd save his eggs for the morning. It was too late to start out now, so they rolled out their blankets and made preparations to bed down for the night. All this time, they hadn't seen a single person.

Early the next morning, the pair set out on the tote road built by George Wright, one of the first European men to traverse the Monashee Mountains. It wound its way out of Eagle Landing, zigging and zagging eastward. The tote road wasn't much wider than a path, wandering through valleys and passes that kept them to the lowest part of the mountains. Contractors used it to haul supplies and equipment for the railway.

Edward enjoyed the glorious scenery, passing by lakes and streams amid the dense forests that lay below the towering mountains, which rose all around him.

As Edward discovered, it took horse and mule power, as well as human labour, to build the railway.

It was hot again, and the bugs and mosquitoes made good meals of Edward, Jim, and the horses. By the end of the day, everyone was exhausted. Edward and Jim threw down their blankets under some trees and slept soundly — until they were awoken by the coyotes howling. Edward had never heard such sounds before.

By mid-morning the next day they reached the line of railway construction. The whole place was alive with activity. Gangs of Chinese workers were busy with picks and shovels preparing the roadbed for the steel rails, while the supervisors stood back at the edge of the forest, smoking and watching the work. Trees were being cut down, stumps were being blown out by explosives, and men were drilling into rock overhangs so they could be blasted out to make way for the rails.

That was when Edward heard the thunder. He looked into the clear blue sky and wondered where it was coming from. Jim explained that he was actually hearing the echo of nitroglycerine blasts being set off in Eagle Pass. Thousands of tons of rock were being moved to make way for the railway.

Every now and then they came upon a camp made up of tents and log buildings. Twice over the next few days, they got hand-outs from the camp cooks, which kept their bellies full without any need to tap into their own supplies. On the third day, they found themselves outside a crude log shack that stood by itself midway between two camps. A man was lounging on a wooden bench out front.

"You boys all want a drink?" The man was wearing dirty corduroy pants held up by tattered suspenders. Woollen underwear that must have once been white covered his stomach and chest. Edward assumed that he was inviting them to have a drink of water.

"Ain't got no water here," the man corrected him. "Just good whisky — made it myself."

Edward realized that this was one of the bootleggers he'd heard infested the route along the railway. As well as selling liquor, the shack would probably be set up for gambling, if it was like other places that Jim had described. He'd explained that whisky was not allowed to be sold within twenty miles on either side of the railway.

Courtesy Revelstoke Railway Museum 075120.

Edward came upon this hastily built railway work camp deep in Eagle Pass.

"The North-West Mounted Police come along every now and then and raid any places that ignore the rules," Jim said. "But that don't stop nobody. The bootleggers set up wherever they can find a place to throw up a table and some stools."

Jim told the bootlegger he'd take a shot. He paid twenty-five cents and was handed a small, dirty glass with about an inch of brown liquid in it. He raised it to his lips, cocked back his head, and let the whisky slip down his throat.

"Arrgh, that'll put hair on your chest. Why don't you try a shot?"

Edward knew his father took a drink of whisky sometimes before dinner. He thought there was no reason he shouldn't try a drink.

Handing a coin to the bootlegger, Edward accepted a ration in the same glass from which Jim had just drunk.

As he brought it to his mouth, the smell of the whisky rose to his nostrils. He almost gagged. The only way to get rid of the smell, Edward thought, was to drink the stuff. He took a great gulp, swallowing it all at once.

For an instant, Edward couldn't figure out what was happening to him. His scalp seemed to be lifting itself off his head. His ears rang. His eyes watered. His stomach rebelled.

Edward threw up. The whisky he'd drank spouted out of his mouth, along with various other things, liquid and otherwise, that had been in his stomach.

Jim and the bootlegger laughed uproariously.

"You'll learn, kid," the bootlegger chuckled. "But you'll have to keep it down longer if it's going to do you any good."

"Come on, Edward," Jim said. "We'd better get out of here."

Afterward, Jim apologized to Edward for failing to warn him about the bootlegger's booze.

"That's not real whisky. It's just moonshine that he makes up himself. Rotgut. Don't let that turn you against the real stuff."

Edward still felt queasy. He wasn't sure he'd ever want to try any kind of alcohol again.

Jim thought that they would make better time if they left the construction line and followed Eagle River as it flowed down from Eagle Pass.

After another night in the forest, they came upon Griffin Lake, where a makeshift village had sprung up to cater to the railway workers. They cadged breakfast from a camp cook and debated how best to get to Farwell. The lake was a mile long and they were tempted to cross it on a scow that was being loaded with half a dozen teams of horses pulling wagons loaded with supplies. The scow looked like a big platform floating on the water; four men stood on either side of the scow, each holding a large oar.

"You can come aboard if you each pay a dollar," one of the men told Edward.

"I'd rather take the trail around the lake and save the dollar," Edward replied.

Courtesy B.C. Archives HP075002.

Edward and his friend Jim walked around Griffin Lake, shown here, rather than pay to take a barge across.

The path ran the length of the lake. It rose up and down with the uneven terrain. Sometimes, it even dipped into the edge of the lake before emerging on dry land. Edward wasn't used to riding a horse, and every bit of his body hurt — especially his bottom. He decided to get off and walk the rest of the way. He made his way through a tangle of grass and ferns that came up to his shoulders. Whenever he veered off the path, he found himself walking on a carpet of green moss three or four inches deep. The moss even grew up the sides of trees to their lowest branches.

Ferns and moss didn't bother Edward, but a shrub called the devil's club did. Jim had warned him that its luxuriant green leaves hid sharp needles that could pierce the skin at the slightest brush. Edward's hands were soon raw and swollen from the pricks of its sharp spikes.

They got back on the main path at the end of Griffin Lake and soon came upon Three Valley Lake, named for the three valleys that met at this point. From there, the terrain was easier leading into Eagle Pass, the notch in the mountains that had been discovered by the surveyor Walter Moberly. Without this pass, it would have been impossible to put a railway through the mountains.

As they rode along the river bank, Edward could see the valley narrowing. It soon became just a gap between mountains that rose, sheer and almost completely vertical, for several thousand feet. The mountains were covered with forests of fir, pine, and cedar trees, like a green blanket over the hillsides. He kept his eyes peeled for an eagle, but he never saw one.

It was getting dark when the Columbia River came into sight, far below them in the distance. The river looked wide and deep, but the boys were happy because it meant they would soon be in Farwell, which was on its east bank. But first, there was one more obstacle to be faced: how to get across the river?

Edward was overjoyed when he saw that a rough wooden bridge had been erected across the Columbia. His happiness faded when the toll keeper told him it would cost twenty-five cents for himself, and another twenty-five cents for his horse.

"Everybody's out to get rich from this railway," Edward complained, before paying the man.

I'm just about out of money. How will I pay for my ticket to the Prairies? Perhaps I can get work in Farwell. Just long enough to earn what I'll need until I join the militia.

Edward was worried that he had heard no news of the fighting anywhere along his journey. He hoped he was not too late to help put down the Rebellion and wished he knew what was happening on the other side of the mountains.

"Maybe the militia's been wiped out," Edward said to Jim. "Just like General Custer and his men at Little Bighorn in '76. Nary a one survived."

Jim looked at him quizzically. "Our men aren't as foolish as that Custer."

"Maybe not. But if I don't get to the Prairies soon, I'll miss everything.

The Town with Two Names

Arthur Stanhope Farwell thought he had put his name on a place, as well as having earned himself a place in history, by founding a settlement, which he named after himself: Farwell, British Columbia. Instead, his efforts earned him only a footnote in the history books.

Arthur Stanhope Farwell was born in Derbyshire, England, the son of a clergyman. He learned to survey land and lay out routes for streets and roads. When he got to British Columbia he was hired as surveyor general, and when a wagon road was needed to move supplies from Eagle Landing on Shuswap Lake to the Columbia River, he was sent out to survey the way.

Farwell knew he was in on something good. He figured out where the CPR would have to cross the Columbia River, and he got a grant from the British Columbia government for over a thousand acres. Then he got busy laying out the townsite of Farwell, never suspecting that he'd be outwitted by the railway.

When Edward landed in Farwell, the straggly little mountain outpost was home to only a few hundred people and residents were anxiously awaiting the arrival of the railway. Workers were laying tracks through the Selkirk Mountains, and the outpost on the Columbia River was smack on its route.

After agreeing to pay Farwell to use his property for a station, the railway company took possession of a large area of flat land half a mile east of Farwell. This land was within the Railway Belt, the strip of territory across the country that Ottawa gave the CPR in return for building the line.

George Stephen, the president of the CPR, decided the town needed a different name. In 1886, he chose to rename the town Revelstoke in honour of Lord Revelstoke, a British businessman who had invested in the railway.

The dispute between Arthur Farwell and the railway didn't end there. The Dominion government refused to recognize provincial land grants, and British Columbia refused to recognize Dominion land grants. Arthur Farwell sued the Dominion government for the rights to his land. Meanwhile, no one in Farwell could get clear title to their land. Many banks and other businesses refused to set up shop in a town where property rights were such a mess.

It wasn't until 1894 that Farwell won his land title, less parts of his grant that the Dominion government had given to others. He was fed up by this point, though, and moved further south to Nelson, British Columbia.

Revelstoke was finally incorporated in 1899, and the big task, making up the lost years when nobody knew who owned what around what had been Farwell, began.

CHAPTER 5

NO TIME TO FIGHT

The boards in the wooden bridge across the Columbia River creaked and groaned with every step, as Edward and Jim, leading their horses, made their way to the far side and into Farwell. The new lumber in the bridge was still green, so it squeaked and snarled when walked on.

"If you'd been here last winter," Jim said, "we'd have crossed the river on an ice bridge. They just lashed a bunch of trees together and let them freeze up in the ice. So solid that teams of horses could cross over on them."

The first thing Edward saw in Farwell was the burned out shells of buildings along Front Street. Tall spires of blackened trees stood like forlorn statues, their branches having been consumed by flames. Dozens of tents lined both sides of the street, mixed in among the wooden frames of new buildings that were being hastily thrown up. He stepped around bits of blackened wood and ash that still littered the roadway.

Courtesy McCord Museum Montreal, I-9045.1.

A figure of controversy, A.S. Farwell gave his name on the place where the railway crossed the Columbia River. The settlement of Farwell was later renamed Revelstoke.

"Guess I forgot to tell you about the fire," Jim told Edward. "Pretty near the whole place burned down in May. These wooden buildings burn like match boxes. But they're building 'er up again. Old Art Fartwell — that's what I call him — started this place. Got himself over a thousand acres of Crown land. Expects to make a lot of money selling it off when the railway gets here."

Farwell stood about halfway between the two sections of the railway. To the east, the track gangs were struggling day and night under the merciless urging of the CPR's general manager, William Van Horne. They were still some distance away in the Selkirk Mountains. To the west, Andrew Onderdonk's navvies were struggling to blast a right of way through Eagle Pass, in the Monashee range.

That night, Edward and Jim slept on the river bank behind the Columbia Hotel. Neither wanted to pay the fifty cents that the innkeeper, Mrs. Clarke, had demanded for a room. The night was warm, the mosquitoes weren't too plentiful, and Edward had no trouble dropping off to sleep.

Daylight in Farwell came on at about five o'clock in the morning. The air had chilled during the night, and Edward awoke to find frost on the ground. He rolled his bedclothes together, gathered up his satchel, and said goodbye to Jim, who had business to attend to. The last Edward saw of him was when he led his two horses to a stable with the sign, Horses bought and sold.

I've come this far, Edward thought to himself, *but I've still a ways to go if I'm going to help put down the Rebellion. I've got miles to go before I reach the end of the line where I can catch a train to the Prairies.*

Front Street was alive with men coming and going from the tents and log shacks on either side of the road. Boats were already moving on the river, carrying men and supplies

Courtesy Revelstoke Railway Museum c75120.

Railway navvies pose with the driver of a wagon team bringing supplies to a camp in the Monashee Mountains in 1885.

to the gold mines up in Big Bend Country. Edward went into a small café that was filled with hungry men being served by a Chinese cook. *All these places seem to be run by Chinese*, Edward thought as he gobbled up a plate of eggs and burnt toast.

He had arrived at just the right time. Two men were talking about the load they had to cart east to the railhead. He heard one say that they could use some help leading their pack horses into the Selkirks.

Edward put down his cup of coffee and went over to where they were sitting. "I've just come through Eagle Pass," he told them. "Did it on horseback. I want to get to the end of track. Let me come along with you and I'll work for my grub."

"Yer justa kid," muttered one of the men.

"Doesn't matter," the other chimed in. "Iff'en he can hold the pony's leash, he'll help us reach the pass."

The man was referring to the Rogers Pass, the narrow opening that Major Albert Rogers had found in the Selkirk Mountains between Farwell and Golden, on the western slope of the Rocky Mountains. Without the pass, the railway would have had to go much further north, where the mountains were lower and less rugged.

The trio set off — with one of the men grumbling about Edward, while the other offered encouragement. It took four days of steady hiking through the mountains to reach the railway workers' advance camp.

Edward's two companions were George Lafferty and Johnny Nelson. They'd been running supplies up the Columbia to the gold camps around Big Bend. But they couldn't resist getting in on the easy money to be made carrying supplies to the railway camps.

As they travelled, Edward started to feel that he was proving his worth. There was the time, for example, that the whole pack train might have tumbled into a canyon if he hadn't held firmly to the lead horse's line.

The railway workers' tents and shacks were set up on a bank of the Illecillewaet River that flowed from Rogers Pass down into the Columbia River. As soon as they arrived, Edward

Surveyors like Major Albert Rogers had to clamber over high peaks to find their way through British Columbia's mountains.

The Secret Pass

Albert Bowman Rogers wanted to make history. And he did, finding the pass through the Selkirk Mountains that became the route for the Canadian Pacific Railway into British Columbia.

Albert Rogers, born in the United States, was an eccentric, tobacco-chewing, hard-swearing man, and a controversial figure — and he was famous for his bushy, white whiskers. Canadian engineers resented his presence. But his superiors praised him for his determination. As a surveyor for the CPR, Rogers had his work cut out for him: he had been told that no route through the Selkirk Mountains existed.

One day, however, he thought he saw a pass in the distance that looked like it might lead to a valley on the other side. Rogers had to give up when his supplies ran out twenty-nine kilometres short of his goal. But he returned twice before finally succeeding on July 24, 1882. That day, he stood in a mountain-ringed meadow on the bank of the Illecillewaet River, which led down to the south-flowing Columbia River. He had found Rogers Pass.

His boss, J.J. Hill, later hired him to help survey the route for his Great Northern Railway in the United States. Rogers was badly injured in a fall from his horse while working in Idaho. He died from cancer in 1889.

and his companions headed straight for the cook house, a large tent distinguished by a tall tin stovepipe giving off a constant stream of smoke. They ate freshly caught river trout, along with steak and vegetables that had been hauled in from Calgary, the nearest town of significant size east of the Rocky Mountains.

Courtesy Revelstoke Railway Museum 03476.

The railway had to cross many ravines and rivers. This bridge spanned the Illecillewaet River. The river roared down into the Columbia River, and the two merged at the site of present-day Revelstoke.

Courtesy Revelstoke Railway Museum 01137.

The Stoney Creek Bridge is one of the most spectacular bridges on the CPR's main line. Measuring 183 metres long, it lies within Glacier National Park in the Rocky Mountains.

After a night in a bunkhouse with twenty railway workers, and with an enormous breakfast tucked into his stomach, Edward set about getting himself a seat on one of the work trains going back to Calgary. Coming in, the trains carried rails, spikes, dynamite, and other equipment and supplies for the railway workers; returning, they ran mostly empty. As the group Edward had arrived with was under contract to the railway, he had no trouble talking himself into a seat in the train's only boxcar.

Sitting on a long bench that ran the full length of the car, Edward watched through an open window as the work train slowly puffed its way up to Rogers Pass. It eventually arrived at the summit, where he could look down into the Beaver River valley.

Edward saw a series of bridges that cut across deep chasms. One especially caught his attention: it was the wooden trestle over Stony Creek that carried the track several hundred feet above the valley floor.

Once over the bridge, Edward could tell by the easy roll of the boxcar that the train was coasting downhill. Before long, the green Columbia River came into sight. It was running north, flowing along a deep chasm gouged out in the Rocky Mountain Trench. Eventually the river would make a giant hairpin turn and head south, back past Farwell. But Edward's train was chugging north, toward the headwaters of the river. In another few hours it pulled into a makeshift station. The station was called Golden, where the Kicking Horse River joined the Columbia.

"Why do they call the river Kicking Horse?" Edward asked the man sitting opposite him.

"Because a horse kicked a fellow in the gut and they thought he was dead," the man answered. "When they went to bury him, he sat up, as alive as could be. So they called the stream Kicking Horse River."

Edward hardly believed the story but he thought it'd be a good one to remember.

Everybody seemed to be getting off the boxcar, so Edward followed. He found out the train crew would be sleeping in Golden overnight before continuing to Calgary in the morning. There was a cook shack near the station and Edward set out for it, thinking he could get a free meal.

But when he got there, he found out that dinner would cost him fifty cents. This wasn't a railway mess car, but a private café owned by Wan Lee, the first Chinese man to settle in Golden.

"You pay, you eat," he told Edward. Hungry, Edward decided he had better pay. What he got for his money was much more than he had expected.

While Edward chewed on a tough piece of meat, a burly man in blue overalls and a railway cap on his head came into the café and sat down beside him. He spread out a newspaper on the counter and began to read aloud the headlines.

"Riel surrenders," the man read aloud. "Rebellion is over. Big Bear taken prisoner."

Edward couldn't believe what he was hearing. Craning to see the small print on the front page of the *Calgary Herald, Mining and Ranch Advocate* Edward's eyes confirmed what his ears had heard. The North-West Rebellion was over!

"You're awful interested in this paper," the man said to him. "It just came in on the train. Filled with news of the Rebellion. What's it to a young fellow like you?"

Edward was so shocked by what he'd heard and read that he hardly knew what to say.

"I didn't think it would be over this soon," Edward told the man. "I was on my way to join the militia. Thought I should get in on the trouble."

"Well, it's all over," the man repeated. "You're too late. The fighting's done."

"I'm surprised it's over so soon," Edward said. "What do you think will happen now?"

The man glowered at Edward. "Don't ya know anything, kid? They'll hang Riel and all his gang. I didn't do ten years in the U.S. Army without learning what an army does when it wins. It takes out its frustrations on whoever it's whupped."

The man, it turned out, was Lieutenant James W. Jeffries (retired), who was only too eager to educate Edward about the ways of armies, politicians, and anybody who gets in their way.

"Why, Canada never had an army until the North-West Rebellion," the old soldier said. "You just had the Royal Navy sitting out there off Halifax and Victoria. You even had an

Englishman, name of General Middleton, commanding what you had for a militia. Three thousand militia came west on the CPR to fight Riel. Took nine days from Montreal to the Qu'Appelle Valley.

"It went like this," Jeffries continued. "They had orders to stamp out Métis and Indian resistance. They got their butts kicked at Duck Lake and Cut Knife Creek. Turning point came at the Battle of Batoche. But only because the Indians used up all their ammunition and Riel had to surrender. His Métis general, Gabriel Dumont, ran off to the States."

Jeffries went on to tell Edward what he'd read in the paper: that the last shots in the Rebellion had been fired by Steele's Scouts, the unit of the North-West Mounted Police commanded by Colonel Sam Steele. His men encountered Chief Big Bear's retreating Cree at Loon Lake. This was the bunch that had held Amelia McLean and other civilians from Fort Pitt prisoner for seventy days. The Calgary paper had more about her and her family. Edward wondered how a girl like Amelia would have dealt with being held prisoner by the Natives.

"Riel's been charged with high treason," Jeffries said, pointing to an article in the paper. "The trouble with the Indians is over. Everything'll go on just as the government wants. The railway'll get millions of acres for its trouble. White settlers will get their choice of home-steads. Those poor bloody Indians, and their half-breed Métis, will be left to starve. Just as well you're not part of it, boy."

Edward felt deflated. There was no time left to fight. He also felt ashamed. Ashamed because he'd told everyone, including his friends from school, that he was going to help put down the North-West Rebellion. He didn't understand much about the causes of the Rebellion, or the injustices that the Métis and the Native people of the Prairies had been forced to endure. He had just wanted the excitement of the action, serving Queen and Country. It was a natural enough feeling for a young man just turned eighteen.

What do I do now?

Edward pondered his choices. He could take the train the next morning to Calgary in the hope that he still might be able to enlist in the militia. He could run back to Victoria, confessing defeat in his great adventure. Or he could look for fresh adventure along the route of the Canadian Pacific Railway as it pressed its way through the uncharted wilderness of mountainous British Columbia.

Edward was both tired and discouraged when he dragged himself to the Golden Hotel, a two-storey wooden building that was the largest on the town's main street. For twenty-five cents, he got a bed in a dormitory with a dozen other men. By now, Edward had become accustomed to the rough ways and crude talk of the men he met along his travels. He put his satchel under his pillow, closed his eyes, and fell fast asleep.

He awoke with a start the next morning as the men stirred around him, complaining of a poor night's sleep, and muttering

The locomotives that pulled construction trains had their own names. This engine was the *Kamloops*.

about what the coming day might have in store for them. He felt the need for fresh air, and was only too glad to escape the stuffy dormitory ahead of most of his roommates. By the time he'd reached the street he was feeling better, but he still didn't know what he was going to do. He kept thinking about his options. In the bright light of the morning, the idea of joining the militia held less appeal than it had the day before. He dreaded the thought of going home and facing his family and friends without some great accomplishment to talk about.

After a while, Edward found himself in front of the small building that served as the railway station in Golden. He saw a locomotive tugging a chain of flatcars carrying steel rails. It was bound for the end of the rails lying between Golden and Farwell. *I could get aboard right now, and be in Farwell by tomorrow morning. There's lots going on there,* he thought. *If I get my oar in before the railway construction's done in the fall I might be able to fix myself up for the winter.*

At the last moment, just as the engineer pulled on the throttle to send more steam to power the big engine, Edward made his decision. The train was chugging faster now. He threw his satchel onto the last flatcar and clambered aboard, clinging desperately to the pile of steel rails it carried. He had to hang on, all the way through Rogers Pass and back to where he'd started from.

I've been a fool. Wasted my time, Edward thought as the train gathered speed. *What's going to become of me?*

The Beavermouth Station as it looked in the 1880s. The workers who built the station went months without pay when the CPR ran short of money.

Courtesy Revelstoke Railway Museum 00661.

70

CHAPTER 6

EDWARD GETS HIS CHANCE

Black puffs of smoke billowed from the stack of the locomotive as the train carrying Edward made its way out of the Columbia River Valley and into the Selkirk Mountains. The newly laid tracks hadn't firmly settled into the railbed, and Edward's spine rattled with every dip and turn of the train. He wiped specks of coal dust from his eyes and, holding his hat in his hand, brushed cinders out of his hair. The ride reminded him of the forest fire that had caught him on the bank of the Fraser River when he he'd first set out for the Prairies.

At first, as the train followed the line up the Beaver River from where it joined the Columbia, it travelled fairly quickly. Before long, however, the train began to grind its way along S-shaped switchbacks, which added many miles to the journey. The switchbacks were the only way the train could edge its way up the sides of mountains, gaining only a bit of altitude at each turn. Edward could look back over the country he'd descended into only the day before, but he worried about slipping off the flatcar. The fear of falling made him cling tightly to the stack of rails he was sitting on.

As the day wore on and the train worked its way farther into the mountains, Edward became more and more entranced at the beauty of his surroundings. Green forests carpeted the lower elevations and, from time to time, he could make out creeks tumbling wildly down the slopes. Going through the Rogers Pass, Edward could see where great slides of stone had

Courtesy B.C. Archives I-30859.

Andrew Onderdonk harnessed his own team of oxen to haul in rail ties and remove stones and bush.

scraped bare the near-vertical walls of the mountains. He could make out, at the very tops of the highest mountains, splotches of snow that still clung to their peaks, even in mid-July.

It was nearly evening when the train met up with the construction workers, who were still laying track at a rate of a mile on a good day or only a few hundred feet on a bad one. The train shunted to a stop not far beyond where Edward had boarded a different train just the day before. Building a railway was slow going in these mountains.

Edward jumped down from the flatcar when a gang of men approached to unload the rails. He heard them say that they'd been held up by lack of track. Another group of workers was putting wooden ties into place to hold the rails and horses and oxen were hauling supplies to tents around the campsite. Edward noticed the two cartage men he'd travelled with from Farwell; he was surprised that they hadn't yet gone back.

"Well lookee, lookee," the unfriendly one said when he saw Edward. "So yer back? Thought you were goin' to fight the Redskins!"

Edward answered as coolly as he dared. "The Rebellion's over, Riel's surrendered, didn't you know?"

The pair continued to chide him for not getting to the Prairies in time to see any action. This was the very sort of thing Edward was afraid he'd have to face at home if he went back to Victoria now.

They grew tired of teasing Edward soon enough, and asked him if he'd like to return with them to Farwell. They were heading back in the morning and Edward was glad to accept their offer.

Although he'd only been away from Farwell for a week, Edward was excited by the changes he saw in the town when the cartage men led their ponies to the Farwell Stables the next day. Buildings that were but bare frames when he'd left now had walls and roofs; and new ones were being started. There weren't as many men living in tents, either. But the biggest change was a freshly painted brown building standing by itself at the end of Front Street. Hanging from it was a sign, POST OFFICE.

Edward suddenly felt homesick and decided to write a letter to his parents. He had paper in his satchel, so he withdrew a sheet, propped his satchel on a flat stone, and began to write:

Dear Mother and Father,

The news here is all about Riel giving up and the Rebellion being put down. I am in Farwell. It is about halfway between the two ends of the railway. As I did not get to fight, I am not ready to come home. I will see what I can find here. I am well, and send my love to everyone.

Your loving son,

Edward

Through the open post office door Edward could see a tall, balding man wearing thick glasses standing behind a counter. *He must be the postmaster*, Edward thought.

"I've written a letter to my folks but I don't have anything to put it in. Can you send it for me?"

The man shoved an envelope at him and extracted a stamp from a box on the counter. Edward paid a penny for the stamp and two pennies for the envelope, which he carefully addressed to his home on Simcoe Street in Victoria. When Edward asked when it would be sent, the man simply looked at him.

"Well, that depends on when I can get someone to carry the mail," he finally answered, after a long pause. "Nobody wants to do it. Not enough in it for them. The railway's paying too much money, or there's always the gold mines up the Columbia. Just can't get any help to make this town into something."

This launched the man into a long tirade against the CPR, the saloonkeepers who were extracting the wages of the railway workers, and the high prices being asked for the remaining empty lots on Front Street.

Edward asked the man what had brought him there.

"Well, I'm the postmaster in charge of this office. Name's Tom Gordon. Not sure what I'm doing here. Guess I'm just another of the old fools who thought they'd find gold in the Columbia."

Wherever the trains ran, a mail car like this CPR Car No. 1 followed. Carrying the Royal Mail was an essential part of the CPR's business.

Courtesy Revelstoke Railway Museum c74936.

Mr. Gordon told Edward that he'd worked for the Post Office Department at Lake Louise — "Prettiest place in the Rockies." He'd been told to follow the railway into British Columbia, and to run a post office wherever the track ended. With the railway approaching Farwell, he had come here to open up a sub-Post Office. But he didn't have anyone to carry mail back through Eagle Pass to Eagle Landing. So he couldn't tell Edward when his letter might be on its way.

"I'm sorry about that," Mr. Gordon said. "Your letter will just have to wait."

Edward listened with mounting excitement. He quickly realized this might be the chance he was looking for.

"I've come up from Eagle Landing," He didn't mention that he'd also gone as far east as Golden. "I made it all the way by horseback. I know the route. I could carry the mail for you."

"How old are you, lad?"

"I'm eighteen. I was going to join the militia but the Rebellion's been put down, so I'm available. I could help you out, at least until the railway's finished."

Edward could tell he'd caught Mr. Gordon's interest.

"The Rebellion, eh? Good for you, lad. Too bad it all ended so soon." He warned Edward that the job would only last a couple of months. And while he could supply him with a horse, he couldn't pay him anything. "It would be like being in business for yourself. See what else you can carry, make it pay the best way you can."

Edward knew Mr. Gordon was taking advantage of him. He'd have to pay wages to an adult. And he'd seen railway workers pay the cartage men to carry stuff for them.

Edward had heard about the famous Pony Express riders in the United States, who, before the railway was built down there, carried mail three thousand kilometres from Missouri to California. The Pony Express riders changed horses every few hours as they rode madly across the Prairie. Edward could imagine himself in this romantic image. It would be really exciting, and give him plenty to talk about when he got home. But he'd have to take his time going back and forth between Farwell and Eagle Landing, since he'd only have one horse and the trip would take two or three days each way.

Mr. Gordon arranged with Mrs. Clarke for Edward to have a room at the Columbia Hotel. It would cost three dollars a week, and was just big enough to hold a mattress, a table, and a chair.

The next morning, Edward went to the stables where Mr. Gordon said there would be a horse for him. He found Blackie in the paddock behind the stable. Edward had never seen an animal quite like this one. True to his name, Blackie had such a dark brown coat that it was almost black, fitted over a short and stocky body. He had short, thick legs with very large hooves, and a long, pointed nose. Edward soon found out that Blackie put his nose to good use by snuffling into his coat pocket to retrieve whatever treats might be there.

"Take good care of that animal," the stable master told Edward. "He's descended from a long line of wild horses. That's why he's built the way he is. To paw through the snow for

Courtesy B.C. Archives I-30817.

Edward was hired to carry mail by horseback from Farwell, on the Columbia River, to Eagle Landing.

grass and work his way through muskeg and over deadfalls. But he's strong, and he'll get you to Eagle Landing without breaking a sweat."

Mr. Gordon gave Edward a saddlebag of mail for delivery, complete with his letter home. Before leaving town, Edward went in and out of stores and saloons offering to take out parcels or bring back newspapers. He collected cash in advance, and set out from Farwell with more than three dollars. *This is going to be a good business.*

By the time he got to Eagle Pass, Edward wasn't so sure he had made the right decision. He had trouble keeping Blackie on the trail, and the mosquitoes and horse flies buzzed around him without mercy. That night, he listened to the howls of wolves and wondered whether bears might be lurking near where he slept.

He cheered up when he rode into the railway camp at Griffin Lake the next afternoon. A long line of low huts had been put up for the workers. The huts had no windows and no ventilation. Men from every country in Europe slept side-by-side like bees in a hive — except when they were arguing, fighting, or getting drunk, which was most of the time.

Edward had just finished his supper when a brawl broke out. A big Swede hit an Italian man, and all the other men quickly went to the aid of their countrymen. Pretty soon all the Swedes were fighting all the Italians, while the few English workers just hung back, laughed, and urged them on.

The railway bosses must have known there would be fights like this. They'd taken care to post a doctor to the camp, and what with attending to men injured in construction accidents and those hurt in brawls, the doctor was left with very little spare time. The only people he didn't tend to were the Chinese, who lived off by themselves in tents some distance from the White camp. The doctor never went there.

The work of building the railway went on day and night, and Edward was amazed at the speed of the construction. He decided to rest the next day and spent hours watching workers build a one-hundred-foot-long truss bridge across a deep chasm. Edward watched the men drag timber to the edge of the chasm and thrust the beams out into empty space, supported by vertical iron rods that connected with overhead struts, which provided the tension to hold the deck in place. The bridge was an engineering marvel. Edward had heard the workers talk about tension and compression and somebody said it was a Howe truss bridge that was being built. It was all finished by supper time, and it wouldn't be long before the first train would pass over it.

When Edward arrived at Eagle Landing, it looked no different than it had on his first visit, and he had no desire to stay there any longer than necessary. He delivered his mail to the post office, picked up a supply of newspapers from New Westminster and Victoria from the *Peerless*, which had just docked, fed his horse, and left town.

Edward found himself back in Farwell on payday; the railway workers were paid in cash. Most headed for the closest saloon or gambling hall, where they played games like Faro or Stud Horse Poker. Others made visits to a type of place Edward had never known existed, places like Irish Nell's. He'd heard them referred to as "hostess houses," but wasn't sure what went on in there. Over the next few days, though, he noticed pretty girls going in and out, and started to get the picture.

One night, Edward was lying on his bed in his tiny room when he heard shots in the street. Looking out the small window, he saw North-West Mounted Police galloping up and down the street. He hurried downstairs.

"What's happening?" Edward asked the hotel night clerk.

"Two men got themselves shot in the gambling hall. Whoever picked them off escaped out the back door. Probably off down the river by now."

The police were riding around trying to find the gunman. *This is too good to miss,* Edward thought, and went out onto the wooden sidewalk in front of the hotel. Suddenly, a figure emerged from the shadows and grabbed him.

"Drop your gun," a voice ordered, while the arm holding him tightened its grip.

"I haven't got no gun! It's just me, Edward the dispatch rider."

"What are you doing out here? We've got enough trouble without looking after you." It was big Ed Ruddick of the North-West Mounted Police. "If it's not those damn gamblers shooting each other, we've got those Provincials to worry about. You're not helping any."

Edward knew Constable Ruddick was referring to the troubles between the Mounties and the British Columbia Provincial Police assigned to Farwell. Instead of working together, they were trying to outdo each other in controlling the liquor trade.

Whisky Traders and Rebellion

The North-West Mounted Police rode to the Prairies in 1874 with orders to keep the peace among Indians, Métis, and the Whites flooding into the region. Because of the work of the NWMP, the Canadian West never experienced the lawlessness that became so common in the American West. Their early activity covered everything from stopping whisky traders to putting down a rebellion.

Colonel Samuel Steele, born in Orillia, Ontario, became one of the most celebrated North-West Mounted Police officers. He led expeditions across the Prairies, fought in the North-West Rebellion, kept order along the Canadian Pacific Railway in British Columbia, and saw duty in the Yukon after the gold rush of 1898. His name is preserved in Fort Steele which was an NWMP outpost and is today a heritage town near Cranbrook, British Columbia.

While on the March West in 1874, Sam Steele wrote in his diary about the Métis, mixed blood people who would later be key figures in the North-West Rebellion:

"The Métis here made a living by hunting buffalo, fishing and freighting. They sowed their crops in the spring, and never saw them again until harvest. If the crops failed it did not matter, for the distance to the herds of buffalo was not far, and the numerous lakes of white fish were near at hand."

Little did he realize that the buffalo herds would soon be wiped out and it would no longer be possible to survive without growing crops.

The North-West Mounted Police got their Royal designation in 1904 and the force merged with the Dominion Police in 1920 to become the Royal Canadian Mounted Police.

Constable Ruddick was in the middle of it all. One of his men had seized sixteen dozen bottles of beer from a liquor dealer; the dealer happened to be friendly with the Provincial Police. A Provincial Police constable took back the beer and arrested the Mountie who had nabbed him. In retaliation, the Mounties jailed the Provincial man. Then the Provincials captured the chief of the North-West Mounted Police post along with two of his constables. A few days later, they were let out of jail and left town.

Not long after that incident, a new squad of North-West Mounted Police arrived in Farwell, commanded by Colonel Sam Steele. Word of his exploits in the capture of Big Bear's men, the feat that ended the North-West Rebellion, had preceded him. The first lot of Mounties was sent away, except for Constable Ruddick, and Colonel Steele ordered his men to restrict themselves to protecting railway property and leave control of the liquor trade to the Provincial police.

The Mounties had their hands full bringing justice to outlaws who lurked along the railway waiting for men to pass by, their pockets filled with money from their summer's labour.

Edward heard tales of many men being held up and relieved of everything they'd earned; some were even killed. A few of the outlaws were hanged, on orders of the fearsome Judge Matthew Begbie. He had brought peace to the gold mining camps, and returned now and then from Victoria, where he now lived.

"Go up before Begbie," the outlaws agreed, "and you'll hang."

Edward worried that he might someday encounter a gang of robbers on his ride through Eagle Pass. He lay awake at night trying to figure out what he'd do.

CHAPTER 7

EDWARD MEETS THE HANGING JUDGE

Edward's fear of encountering a gang of robbers began to melt away as the days passed without incident. Until, that is, the day when something extraordinary happened to him as he rode along an especially lonely section of the trail.

He suddenly found his way blocked by three gnarled men with guns at their hips.

"Get down offen that horse, boy," one of them commanded. He was a coarse looking brute.

Edward slid off the horse. One of the man's partners ordered Edward to hold Blackie's reins. The bandits made him empty his pockets. He held out the bits of change he had, which amounted to less than two dollars.

Edward knew that wouldn't satisfy the thieves. They'd want to loot the saddle bags strapped to Blackie, which contained the mail and other packages he was carrying. He decided he couldn't let that happen and used the plan he'd come up with when he'd been

Photo by James Hunt, 1860. Courtesy B.C. Archives A-01098.

Judge Matthew Begbie imposed the death penalty so often he became known as "the Hanging Judge."

worrying about what to do if he was ever held up.

Edward gave Blackie a good slap on the rump. *Whump!*

Off Blackie took, carrying the mail with him. The three highwaymen soon forgot about Edward. They leapt back on their horses and took off after Blackie. But as Edward would find out when he finally got back to Farwell, they never caught up to him. Blackie had casually found his way back to the stable, unconcerned about his romp in the forest. The saddlebags were untouched.

Edward reported the hold up to Constable Ruddick.

"Damn ruffians," the policeman muttered. "Trying to rob the Royal Mail — that's a hanging offence."

That night, while wandering past the swinging doors of the Columbia Hotel saloon, Edward heard his name being called. It was Constable Ruddick.

"Come in here. There's somebody who wants to meet you."

Before Edward knew it, he was looking up into the face of Judge Matthew Begbie who happened to be in Farwell, having taken a break from his duties in Victoria as chief of the British Columbia Supreme Court.

"They tell me you're a brave young man," Judge Begbie said to Edward. "If those ruffians who held you up had gotten away with the mail, we'd have put the Mounties, as well as the Provincials onto them. And I bet they'd have got them, too. I've not the slightest doubt. Three more I would have had to hang."

Judge Begbie congratulated Edward on his quick thinking in sending his horse off before the bandits could get the mail.

"A smart young fellow like you is going to make out all right in this country."

Judge Begbie made Edward feel proud. But he frightened him, too. A man with so much power, a man who could put an end to a person's life for just about any reason, was a man to stay away from. As soon as he could politely make his departure from the judge's presence, Edward did so.

Ambling down the street, Edward decided the time had come for him to have a look at one of the hostess houses. He still wasn't exactly sure what went on there, but he thought that if they rented out rooms, he might get a better place than the tiny room he was living in at the Columbia Hotel.

At one of the houses, he saw a red-headed woman standing at the door. *She must be Irish Nell*, he thought. He'd heard she was tough as nails, but that she had a heart of gold.

"Good evening, young man," Irish Nell greeted him. "Would you like to come in and look around?"

Why not, Edward thought. He followed her into a front room that was set out as a parlour. There were easy chairs, a sofa, and gas lamps. A painting of a woman wearing very few clothes hung from one wall.

"Do you have rooms here?" Edward asked.

"Something better," Irish Nell told him. "Follow me."

In the next room, Edward saw two of the girls that he'd noticed on the street earlier that day. He saw that both had their faces painted and were wearing what looked like the corset that he knew his mother put on when she wanted to get all dressed up — except these girls weren't wearing anything over their corsets.

Suddenly, Edward realized he'd been a fool. This was no rooming house: it was one of those places where men went to meet girls.

"Uhh, I don't think so," Edward muttered, his face reddening. He turned and fled.

As he rushed out through the front parlour, Edward noticed three men had come in and sat down while he'd been in the back room. It was the three who had held him up in Eagle Pass!

Edward hurried down the street to the North-West Mounted Police post. He was glad to see Constable Ruddick there.

"I just saw them! The three who held me up. They're over at Irish Nell's."

Constable Ruddick told Edward to stay where he was. Five minutes later, gun in hand, he returned with the three men in tow. They were a sad sight. Gone was the bravado they'd shown when they'd held him up. They filed meekly into the only cell in the small building.

The "Hanging Judge" — or Was He?

Matthew Baillie Begbie was born on a ship but became famous in the gold fields of British Columbia for his stern administration of justice, which earned him the nickname, "the Hanging Judge." But he may have been unfairly tagged: the death penalty was mandatory for murder in his day and, in several cases, he successful argued for clemency and got many killers off with life in jail.

Begbie's parents were aboard a British ship off the Cape of Good Hope, South Africa, when Matthew was born. Educated in England, he was sent to British Columbia in 1858 to be judge in the new colony. He arrived just as the great Cariboo Gold Rush brought thousands of miners to the British Columbia interior. Lawbreakers were intimidated by his reputation and his appearance. He was an imposing man at six feet five inches tall, with white hair and a black mustache, and carried himself with an air of authority.

When Native people in the Chilcotin District killed twenty-one White men who had devastated tribal communities while building a road, Begbie had five of them hanged. During his years as a judge he hanged a total of twenty-seven men for a range of crimes.

Begbie made his views clear when a man charged with murder was let off with manslaughter: "Had the jury performed their duty, I might now have the painful satisfaction of condemning you to death, and you, gentlemen of the jury, you are a pack of Dallas horse thieves."

Begbie became chief justice of British Columbia when the new province joined Canada in 1871. He once jailed an editor who criticized him. The editor, John Robson of the New Westminster paper, the *British Columbian*, later became the premier of British Columbia. Begbie also wrote many of the laws for the new province.

Begbie spent a great deal of time in the interior of the province. He once walked from New Westminster to Lillooet and back, a distance of 563 kilometres, and in one year alone he rode more than 5,000 kilometres.

Despite his fearsome reputation, Begbie championed a lot of progressive legislation. He was highly critical of laws discriminating against Chinese people. He called such laws "an infringement of personal liberty and the equality of all men before the law."

Matthew Begbie was knighted in 1875 and died in 1894. Today, the historic Cariboo district gold mining town of Barkerville, British Columbia honours Judge Begbie's life by staging annual reenactments of his famous trials.

"You go along, Edward, and we'll let you know when we need you."

During the next week Edward made two trips to Eagle Landing, which were both agreeable and profitable trips. He witnessed a number of accidents, many fights, and all sorts of thrills every day — all of which kept the doctors very busy. He happened on an emergency case once, when he found a doctor tending to a worker whose leg had been crushed by a load of rails. Another time, he saw two Chinese men fall from a cliff while they were trying to plant dynamite. Their boss, a White man, ordered them to get up and go to their tents. But Edward couldn't stop thinking about how he would have to testify in court when the robbers came up before Judge Begbie.

Judge Begbie, even though he was now head of the British Columbia Supreme Court, still liked to "ride the circuit" as he had done for years, visiting out of the way mining and railway camps to dispense his brand of rough and ready justice.

Edward found a note waiting for him when he got back to his room one night, telling him to be in court the next morning at nine o'clock. The lobby of the Columbia Hotel served as a courtroom whenever it was needed.

A crowd had already gathered when Edward came down the stairs. Judge Begbie sat behind a large table with Constable Ruddick at his side. The three prisoners waited against the wall, guarded by a man carrying a shotgun.

Edward found himself sworn is as the only witness to the men's crime.

"Can you point out the men who robbed you?" asked Constable Ruddick, whose job it was to question Edward.

"Yes. They're right there." Edward pointed to the men lined up against the wall.

"How much did the men steal from you?"

"I think it was about two dollars. They took all my change."

Edward went on to explain how he had slapped Blackie on the rear and the bandits had ridden off after the horse.

"How do you plead?" Judge Begbie demanded of the men.

"Not guilty," they all replied.

"Nonsense!" the judge bellowed. "You're as guilty as sin. Robbing the Royal Mail is a capital offence and you're all going to hang."

"Oh, Judge Begbie, please don't hang them," Edward pleaded. "They only stole my change. They didn't touch the mail. I don't want them to hang on my account."

Judge Begbie looked startled. He stared at Edward, glanced at the prisoners, and beckoned to Constable Ruddick. They whispered quietly to each other. Judge Begbie cleared his throat, and spoke directly to Edward.

"Edward, you must understand I am obliged to enforce the law. I only hang when hanging is warranted. But … maybe you're right. Maybe they didn't know you were carrying the Royal Mail. So I am going to grant your wish."

Turning to the men, Judge Begbie passed sentence.

"Five years in jail. And if you ever come before me again, it'll be the rope for all of you."

Edward let out a deep breath. He might even have been more relieved than the three men who had just escaped the noose.

CHAPTER 8

LORD LANSDOWNE COMES CALLING

The second most exciting thing that happened to Edward while he was in Farwell — the most exciting being the time he was robbed, of course — was when the governor general, Lord Lansdowne, came to visit. He had been in Canada for two years as the personal representative of Queen Victoria. By all accounts, Lord Lansdowne had taken a great interest in the building of the railway to the Pacific. He was known to be a good horseman with a passion for fishing and all things outdoors. The governor general and his wife got off the train at the end of the track east of Farwell. That night, Lord Lansdowne penned a letter to his mother:

> We travelled from the summit of the Rockies (in railway parlance the point where the railway begins to go downhill) to the end of the track.

Breakfasted in the car at 7:20 and took ponies to resume the journey, rode about 18 miles over fearful ground, but thro' the grandest possible scenery to a railway village called Farwell where we camped very comfortably in tents provided by the Ry. People.

Edward was there for Lord Lansdowne's visit to Farwell in 1885.

Edward followed along with the governor general's party the next day. He stayed just far enough back so as not to be questioned about what he was doing.

At about eight o'clock the regal visitors rode out of Farwell, bound for a First Nations reservation. They were met by a Native man, known as Red Crow, and his principal chiefs, all of whom were on horseback and wearing their finest leather coats topped by feather headdresses.

Lord Lansdowne was escorted to a chair where, surrounded by his staff and the North-West Mounted Police, he sat to receive Red Crow. Red Crow and his chiefs sat on the ground, in a semi-circle, while an interpreter put their words into English. It was mostly complaints about how the government was treating them. After a time, gifts were produced on both sides: a pair of field glasses were handed to Red Crow and pipes, knives, and tobacco were given out to the others.

The Lord Who Loved Canada

Lord Lansdowne was governor general from 1883 to 1888, when the British Empire was at its glory and Queen Victoria's new Dominion of Canada faced many challenges.

Born to an important family, Henry Petty-Fitzmaurice came to Canada at a time when public confidence had been shaken by the Pacific Scandal over the building of the railway, and the country was in a recession. Then along came the North-West Rebellion.

As he travelled about Canada, Lord Lansdowne developed a great fondness for the outdoors, became an avid salmon fisherman, and took part in winter sports. His journey to Farwell (now Revelstoke) in 1885 gave him the opportunity to meet First Nations chiefs and visit outlying points by horseback and boat. He returned to British Columbia after the completion of the railway to travel all the way to Port Moody, which was the end of the line at the time.

Lord Lansdowne inherited a vast estate and was a man of great wealth. He served the British government in many capacities: he was the viceroy of India, then considered the jewel of the British Empire, and returned home to serve as secretary of state for war, and later as Foreign Secretary. He died in 1927 and left an estate worth over one million pounds Sterling (CDN$5 million; today worth about $60 million).

Courtesy B.C. Archives HP057591.

The governor general, Lord Lansdowne, met with the First Nations chiefs of the Shuswap and other tribes in the area when he visited British Columbia.

After the ceremony everyone stood while a bugler sounded "God Save the Queen" and people sang along to the Royal anthem. Edward's chest filled with pride: he'd been brought up to admire Queen Victoria. As a good British boy, he was proud of his connection with the great Empire and the fact that he lived in a place named after his queen.

Then something happened that Edward could never have expected.

Colonel Sam Steele was in charge of the escorts who cleared the way for Lord Lansdowne. When he saw Edward, he pulled up his horse, ordered the procession to halt, and turned to the governor general.

"Your Excellency, I want you to meet a fine young man. Typical of the kind of brave young boys we're bringing up in this country."

Edward was stunned. He didn't think Colonel Steele knew about him. He could only stand and stare as the governor general trotted his horse his way.

"This is the boy who carries the Royal Mail over Eagle Pass. He was held up the other day, but had the presence of mind to send off his mount before they could get at the saddlebags. We caught the ruffians, and they're in the penitentiary by now."

"I see they start them young in Canada," the governor general said. "You've done well, young man. Keep that up and you'll have a bright future. I could use somebody like you in the Horse Guards. Always need good men at my place in Wiltshire, Bowood House."

Bowood House was one of the most stately homes in England, situated amid a two-thousand acre estate, but Edward couldn't have known this.

After Lord Lansdowne's brief word, he spurred on his horse, and the official party rode on.

Edward travelled back to Farwell that night, happy that he would have an exciting tale to tell about his encounter with the governor general in a mountain valley beyond Farwell.

But the governor general wasn't the only remarkable person Edward met during his remaining days in Farwell.

Edward liked to watch the men building the railway. He would stare transfixed, as fifty or sixty men hung on ropes above Summit Lake while they drilled holes in the rock face of the mountain. Their job was to fill the holes with dynamite sticks that had been laced together with a long fuse, which was lit twice a day by the man charged with setting off explosions. When it went off, a tremendous blast would shake Eagle Pass. Hundreds of tons of rock hurtled through the air, coming to rest along the shore of Summit Lake. Sometimes the rock tumbled right into the lake.

Courtesy Revelstoke Railway Museum 00996.

After each blast, swarms of men with shovels and carts moved the loose earth and rock: they were all Chinese and looked like ants, slaving away for the good of the railway.

Edward was riding Blackie the day he met Dukesang Wong, and was anxious to get through before a storm struck. But the blasting held him up, and he noticed that one of the Chinese workers seemed to be giving directions to the work gang. When Edward heard the man speaking in English to the foreman, he decided to ride over and listen to what was being said.

Building tunnels through solid rock was always a challenge for the railway builders.

"Gold Mountain is not as kind to us as we expected. Why can White men go unpunished, when we are punished for no reason and forced to work in the cold, with little food or clothing?"

Edward didn't understand what they were arguing about. When the foreman rode off, he asked the Chinese man where he learned to speak English.

"My teaching master spoke excellent English, and he passed on to me, his poor, stupid student, whatever my small brain could absorb."

Edward decided to choose his words very carefully, since he'd heard that the Chinese were very modest.

"My name is Edward. My poor horse and I ride twice this way every week."

The man's face lit up at Edward's attempt to match the humility and reticence that were distinguishing characteristics of cultivated Chinese conversation.

"I am called Dukesang Wong. I have worked with the railway all the way from New Westminster. It has been hard and terrible work that my countrymen have been given. We will be happy to see the end of the building of this railway."

Edward told Dukesang that he had watched the Chinese workers and thought they were very brave, and eagerly accepted Dukesang's invitation to share a meal.

As Edward followed Dukesang into his tent, he thought back to the days when he ran from Chinese in the back streets of Victoria. *I know better now*, he thought.

"Here, here, sit," Dukesang pointed to a folding chair inside the tent. There were two other men in the tent, who got up and quickly went outside. Dukesang called after them in Cantonese, and one of them came back with a plate of food for Edward. It contained part of a baked fish, rice balls, and a baked bun. Edward ate with his fingers, since he didn't know how to use the chopsticks Dukesang offered him and there was no sign of a knife or fork. Dukesang held his plate close to his face, and expertly used chopsticks to transfer his food to his mouth.

After eating, Dukesang poured cups of tea for himself and his guest. Feeling more relaxed, Edward asked what it was like working for the railroad. He wanted to know how long Dukesang had been in Canada, and what he planned to do when the railway was finished.

"I'll tell you my story, if you'd like to hear it," Dukesang said.

"Oh, yes, I do. Tell me everything."

CHAPTER 9

COURAGE ON GOLD MOUNTAIN

Dukesang took a deep breath and began talking.

"The worst part was last winter. There was no work for me and my gang of thirty. All the construction stopped for the winter, along with our pay, and we were all hungry. Every morning when I awoke, I wondered if I would have to bury another of my men."

Dukesang told Edward that he was the youngest and strongest of the workers, but even he was beginning to suffer from beriberi. It was a terrible disease that the Chinese called black leg; it came from subsisting on a diet of just rice. Dukesang and his men seldom got to eat any vegetables or meat. As the spokesman for his crew, he often complained to the White foreman but it did no good.

One day early in 1885, with the ground still frozen, Dukesang went over to his friend Wing Sun's bed mat. Wing's legs were swollen, and he complained of terrible pains in his chest and his head. Dukesang felt bad that he had no more bok choy, which he had grown in a small wooden box. The leafy green vegetable would have made a good soup to serve his dying friend.

Later that day, Wing breathed his last. The few pennies he had managed to save weren't enough to send his bones back to Saltwater City — the Chinese name for New Westminster — let alone China. Dukesang had to put his body in the forest and wait until the ground thawed enough to bury him.

Railway building stopped during winter, but warmly dressed surveyors pressed on.

"So many of us suffered and died, I cannot count them all. My dying countrymen prefer to spend their last days in the opium shacks. The delirium of the opium at least releases them from their awful hardships. What else could they do? What hope did they have?"

It had been four years since he had joined the six thousand Chinese coolies — as their White bosses called them — who were brought to Canada to build the railway.

"As soon as they heard I could speak some English, they hired me. My countrymen asked me to speak for them. But that did not relieve me of my share of the work. Whether it was carrying nitroglycerine packed in straw or drilling holes in the rock or hauling away the rock after the blasts, I always did my share."

Dukesang was slight of build, with black hair and dark eyes. He had a lively look about him, and was quick to make a joke or laugh.

"I have written it all down in my journal, in Mandarin. I want my children and my grandchildren, when they come into the world, to have this record of all the important things that have happened to me here on Gold Mountain."

Dukesang explained that, as his father's only son, he had enjoyed many privileges but had also carried many responsibilities back home in China. It was up to him to absorb his lessons in writing, astronomy, and geography, and to learn the ways of peace and harmony that were being passed on to him. Most of all, he had to maintain the family honour, which was important above all else.

When he was still a boy, disaster befell his family. Dukesang's father was a government official, a judge who settled disputes over land ownership. In the last case he handled, he rendered a decision that cost a family some of its land, and the family took revenge by bribing a servant to poison him at a banquet.

"My mother was beside herself with grief. She committed suicide. It was a great dishonour to our family. She couldn't be buried in the family cemetery and had to be put to rest in common ground, along with peasants and homeless wanderers. But she left a note for me, which told me to present a good face to the world and to make wise use of my learning."

Dukesang told Edward how he had travelled to the great capital Peking and on to a city on the North China seacoast. There he got a job tutoring the eldest son of the warlord Sen Yutseng.

"One day while I was meditating in the garden, my eyes fell on a beautiful young girl whose name was Lin. She was the daughter of the neighbour, Yin-Ling. She was too young to marry, but Yin-Ling promised me that this girl would some day be my wife."

First, however, Dukesang had to wait for Lin to grow up. This would give him time to gain enough wealth to buy land and a home for his bride. So it was that he decided to travel to North America.

In the summer of 1880, Dukesang boarded a small three-masted wooden ship to sail to Portland, Oregon, along with several dozen peasants who were fleeing famine in the south of China. The voyage cost forty dollars each, and many of the poor, landless peasants had raised the money by signing over their children to wealthy farmers for years as servants.

Tea was served once a day, with a hundred grams of rice per person. Once they'd arrived in Portland, everybody was kept on board for another three weeks until they could be given a clean bill of health.

"One of my countrymen wrote a poem about that time, I will recite it for you:

> Destitute, no fuel or food,
> We borrow money to go abroad.
> No matter what we say or do,
> The customs men won't let us through,
> Like convicts, locked up in some island cell,
> We rail against this unjust hell."

They were finally allowed onshore to take their first look at this strange, foreign land. Dukesang soon discovered that life on Gold Mountain was nothing like he had expected.

After a damp and chilly winter working odd jobs, relying on what fish he could catch in the Columbia River for food, Dukesang heard about the new railway being built further north. He moved to New Westminster and became a navvy on the Fraser River section of the Canadian Pacific Railway.

"I did all the rough jobs, like breaking rock and helping to drill tunnels through the canyon walls over the river."

Edward had seen many Chinese workers moving great piles of rock clad only in sandals and thin cotton pants and blouse, and asked Dukesang why they had such poor clothing.

"We have no money to buy anything better. Sometimes, in winter, we wrap burlap bags around our feet. We work twelve hours a day, six days a week and we're paid seventy-five cents a day. Just half what the White workers get. And we have to provide our own clothing, food, and tools. I had the sad duty of watching many of my friends die. They were just a small number among the hundreds killed by disease and accident."

Dukesang admitted that he often wondered if this huge project to build a railway across Gold Mountain was not just a wild dream, something that would never be accomplished. But he believed that a civilized man could be distinguished from a barbarian by his quiet acceptance of life's misfortunes.

Courtesy Library and Archives Canada NPC C-006686B

Chinese workers, seen in this photo from 1881, faced injury or death every day because of their very dangerous work.

"All the lighter types of work — surveying, supervising the labourers, driving the locomotives — is kept for the Whites. The heavy, dangerous work is left to the Chinese."

Edward asked Dukesang about the rumours of riots he had heard.

"Yes, there have been riots. One day, a foreman refused to pay the wages owed to two workers he had fired. My countrymen hurled rocks at the foreman and his timekeeper and they both showed blood. That night, our camp was attacked by twenty White men. One Chinese man was killed and many hurt. The White doctor refused to treat them."

Picking up his journal, Dukesang translated for Edward an entry he had written.

> So many of us Chinese have suffered and died here recently, I cannot recount them all. But the Western people will not allow any more of us to land here now, although they scold us for not working enough. How these things wear my soul down to nothing. But my words are meaningless, and my speech now falls upon deaf ears and closed eyes. These mighty lands are great to gaze upon, but the laws made are so small.

"The men in my camp all come from remote villages," Dukesang continued, putting his journal down. "They cling to their old ways, keeping their pigtails as a symbol of loyalty to the emperor. They wear their loose coolie jackets, cotton trousers, and flimsy slippers. And most don't even attempt to learn English. Why bother? They think that they will soon have enough money to return to China, to live in comfort on their Gold Mountain dollars. But very few ever will. Most just grow sicker and weaker each year.

"We thought we would never see spring: no rice shipments had come for months."

Finally, a boat from China docked in Saltwater City just in time, bringing with it twelve hundred portions of rice, a month's supply for each man. Soon, the first asparagus shoots made their appearance, and before long Chinese cooks were putting the first green vegetables they had seen in months into their cooking pots.

By the time Edward sat listening to this tale, Dukesang was counting the days until his work would come to an end. He had buried his friend Wing Sun's bones and apologized to his spirit that there wasn't enough money to send his body to Saltwater City.

Many of the labourers who worked with Dukesang planned to go to Victoria. There were many Chinese people there already, and they would be able to live among their countrymen, dreaming of the day when their wives and families could join them. Others had already left the work gangs and had started panning for gold in the Fraser River. So many of Dukesang's countrymen gathered at one place on the river that it came to be known as Chinaman's Bar. But Dukesang told Edward he had other ideas: he had decided that his future lay in Saltwater City. That was where he would go once the railway was finished.

"Maybe I'll be able to marry Lin and bring here to Gold Mountain," Dukesang said. There was a catch in his throat as he spoke.

Edward left Dukesang's tent late that night. As he wandered back to where he had left Blackie safely tethered beside his sleeping bag, he thought about what he had just heard.

A Voice for the Voiceless

Dukesang Wong survived the terrible ordeals the Chinese workers suffered during the building of the CPR and, in his journal, left one of the very few written records by those who had come to Gold Mountain to find their fortune. Through his words, he has given a voice to the voiceless.

He fulfilled his ambition to become a tailor in New Westminster and returned to China to marry his childhood sweetheart Lin and bring her to Canada. He had to pay a fifty dollar head tax before she was allowed into the country. The tax was later increased to five hundred dollars, and further Chinese immigration was prohibited. The head tax was abolished in 1947, and in 2006 the Canadian government apologized for the tax and for mistreatment of early Chinese immigrants.

Dukesang Wong died in 1918. His descendants live on today in British Columbia.

They're just people like us. They want to get this railway built, and then they want to live with their families.

The thought of family made Edward a little sad. But he knew that it wouldn't be long before the Last Spike was driven. There'd be time enough for family after that.

CHAPTER 10

EDWARD RIDES
THE RAILS

The days were beginning to cool and nightfall was coming on early, signalling the approach of autumn in the mountains. Edward felt the chill of a stiff breeze on his face. He buttoned up his jacket as he rode along the tote road from Farwell to Eagle Landing; he had only a few packages of mail and parcels crammed into his saddlebag. A strange stillness had settled over the forest. Construction camps and gambling halls, where the sounds of cursing and carousing had once filled the air, were now silent and abandoned.

Dukesang Wong and his countrymen were finished building the most difficult part of the rail line. They had pushed beyond Summit Lake and were approaching Eagle Pass. It wouldn't be long before they'd meet up with the crews working their way from the East. Those gangs, mostly labourers from eastern Europe, had conquered Rogers Pass and were now almost in Farwell.

As he looked around on his last ride on that late October day, it seemed to Edward as if some scourge had swept through the mountains. Wayside houses were shut up and deserted. He saw dozens of men, laid off by the railway, trudging on foot with all their belongings, headed back to Eagle Landing. Their abandoned camps looked ghostlike at night. The sight gave Edward the shivers as he opened his bedroll and settled down to sleep under a large fir tree.

The thing that stood out the most on this last trip was the way the silence was broken only by the hideous shrieking of construction locomotive whistles as they hurried along, their flatcars loaded with steel rails. The rails fell with a dull clang as they were dropped onto ties, ready for the spikes that would hold them in place.

Edward felt overcome by feelings of sadness and loneliness. Where there had once been the laughter of the gamblers and the shouts of "Stand to!" and "Look out below!" as nitro-glycerine blasts threw tonnes of rock through the air, all was quiet. Edward lay awake for a long time, thinking about everything he had seen and done. He decided it was time to pack things in. He'd made a few dollars and he would have no shortage of stories to tell when he got back to Victoria.

A few days later, Edward returned Blackie to the Farwell Stables. He felt like he was abandoning the best friend of his life. He wrapped one arm around the horse's neck, patted him on the rump, and told him he would never forget him.

There was time for one last walkabout around Farwell. At the post office, he said goodbye to Mr. Gordon and thanked him for the chance he'd given him to carry the mail.

While he was there, the famous Albert S. Farwell wandered in. Mr. Gordon introduced him, but Mr. Farwell didn't seem much interested in young Edward.

Edward knew that Mr. Farwell was fighting with the CPR over where the railway would build its station. He wanted it on his land, but the CPR had other ideas: it had all kinds of property of its own, farther up the hillside from the river. Mr. Farwell said he was going to sue the CPR. Mr. Gordon wished him luck, but warned him that the CPR usually got its way. None of this made much sense to Edward and he slipped quietly out the door while the two men continued to argue.

Walking along Front Street, Edward was amazed at how quickly the town was growing. There was a store selling wine and liquor, and another offering various kinds of jewellery. There were Chinese joss houses, where the railway labourers gathered to burn incense and pray to their gods and ancestors. And, of course, there were the hostess houses, quiet in mid-afternoon. Edward knew they'd be busy that night because it was payday in Farwell.

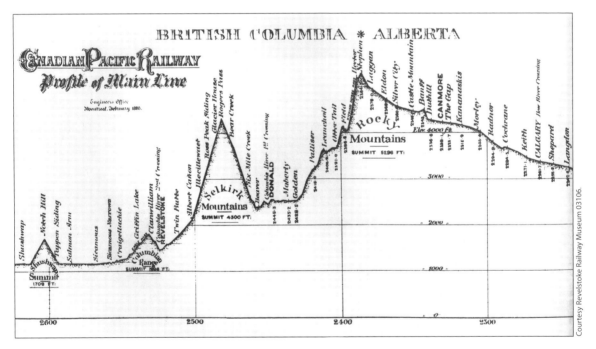

This CPR main line chart shows how the railway line scaled mountain heights and plunged into valleys as it made its way into British Columbia.

There was one thing that always lifted Edward's spirits, and that was the beauty of the mountains around him. He was glad of that that afternoon, as he raised his eyes to the vast glacier that covered most of the great peak towering over the horizon. He was looking at one of Canada's last great glaciers. Unknown to Edward or anyone else at the time, the climate was getting milder after many years of cold weather. In another century, the great glacier Edward was looking at would shrink to one-third its size.

There was one thing Edward was determined to do before he returned home to Victoria: see the completion of the railway. Constable Ruddick had told him there would a ceremonial driving of the Last Spike, and that it would take place in a few days at Craigellachie. Edward decided he would be there.

Trains crossed many trestles similar to this one in Eagle Pass near Craigellachie.

Courtesy Revelstoke Railway Museum 75138.

Edward's spirits lifted again when he saw his old friend.

"Why Mr. Ferguson, I haven't seen you since you got off the boat in Kamloops!"

"That's right, lad, and here we meet up in Farwell."

Edward had all kinds of questions for Mr. Ferguson. "Did you cut all the ties for the railway? How are things at your sawmill? Did you know they're going to drive the Last Spike in a few days?"

Mr. Ferguson chuckled when he heard Edward's questions.

"We delivered the last load of ties yesterday," Mr. Ferguson said. "Dumped them off in Craigellachie. That's where they'll be driving the Last Spike. I've come along for the ceremony."

Edward wondered why the place where the railway was coming together was called Craigellachie. He'd heard people in Farwell throwing around that name, but what was so special about it? There was nothing there but a collection of bunk houses and a pile of steel rails and equipment. He decided to ask Mr. Ferguson if he knew what the name meant.

"Famous place in Scotland, mentioned in a Scottish poem. It's a favourite of George Stephen, the president of the CPR. He likes to quote it. Says the railway, like Craigellachie, will never be moved. Get on with it! Raise the money! Get the line built! Don't be moved! Craigellachie!"

As Edward and Mr. Ferguson were talking, CPR locomotive No. 148 was chugging its way across the prairie, its diamond-shaped smokestack belching puffs of black smoke that vanished into a clear blue sky. It was pulling a cordwood tender, two fancy parlour cars named the Saskatchewan and the Matapedia, a dining car, and a caboose. Aboard were some of the highest officials of the CPR.

The train had set out nearly a week before, from Montreal, for its date with destiny. After years of struggle, political infighting, and financial high wire antics, the railway was only days from being finished.

"They'll all be on that train," Mr. Ferguson told Edward. "I imagine Mr. Smith — that's Donald Smith — will be enjoying a nice bottle of Scotch. There's a man who started out as a fur trader for the Hudson's Bay Company. Worked his way up. One of the big investors in the railway."

Mr. Ferguson asked Edward if he'd ever heard of Sandford Fleming.

Sandford Fleming drew up the first plan for a railway across Canada. For a time he served as chief engineer of the CPR.

He Dreamt the "National Dream"

Sandford Fleming is known as the "father of Standard Time." He is less well-known as the man who first dreamt the dream of the Canadian Pacific Railway.

Even before Confederation, Canada was a country wild about building railways. It was the only way to span the vast distances of this great new land. Fleming had come to Canada from Scotland at the age of eighteen and took up work as a surveyor. He became the chief engineer of three different railways, one in Ontario, the Intercolonial from Montreal to Halifax, and the Canadian Pacific Railway.

In 1862, Fleming had set out a scheme for a "highway to the Pacific." His estimate of the cost, one hundred million dollars, turned out to be right on the mark. Many thought it would be cheaper to go through the United States, but Sir John A. Macdonald felt otherwise.

Macdonald gave the contract to the Canada Pacific Railway Company, organized by Hugh Allan, a Montreal financier, in 1871. Macdonald was forced to resign when it came out that he had taken money from Allan to finance an election campaign in what became known as the Pacific Scandal. After returning to power in the 1879 election, Macdonald pushed ahead with the railway through a new syndicate formed by George Stephen. The first spike was driven at Bonfield, Ontario, a village near North Bay, in 1881.

When Sandford Fleming arrived in Craigellachie for the Last Spike, he was no longer chief engineer. He lost that job when a royal commission blamed him for delay and confusion in the railway's construction. It didn't bother Fleming, though: his idea for standard time around the world had caught on. No longer would every town set its clocks by its own reckoning. The world was divided into twenty-four time zones, with Greenwich, England, as the prime meridian.

"He'll be on the train, too. First man to get the idea of building a railway from coast to coast. Invented standard time, so each little village isn't running its clocks on its own time. A great man."

About the only important person not on the train, Mr. Ferguson said, would be the president of the railway, George Stephen.

"Him and Smith are cousins. But Mr. Stephen's off in England, raising money to finish the line." His quest had been successful: the English banker Edward Baring, of Barings Bank, was advancing them the money.

Edward was one of the first to see the train, with a big number 148 on its front, steam into Farwell. He caught sight of the distinguished passengers as they alighted to walk about the town. Mr. Ferguson was right up there with them, showing them around. Of course, Edward didn't dare speak to any of them.

The train sat on a siding for several days, waiting for the two work gangs to meet each other at Craigellachie. Steady rain turned the thin mountain soil into mud, holding up the last few miles of construction. Edward checked every day for news of the work. Finally, on Thursday, November 6, 1885, word came that the last supply train, consisting of an engine, a tender, and three flatcars loaded with steel rails, would leave that afternoon for Craigellachie. The fateful hook-up would take place the next morning.

Leaving his satchel at the Columbia Hotel, Edward hurried down to the tracks just in time to see the flatcars being shunted into place behind the engine. He saw several men clamber on board. He ran to catch up, and swung aboard the last flatcar just as the train began to pick up steam.

Huddled among the cold rails, he thought of his earlier ride from Golden when he also clung to a flatcar loaded with rails. It had been warm that day, but not today: he was facing a cold, cheerless, and rough ride. A few miles outside Farwell, it started to snow. The snow made the tracks slippery and the train had difficulty making its way up the grade into Eagle Pass.

Three times it ground to a halt before sliding back. Finally, in desperation, the engineer ordered the last car to be cut loose. Edward hurried to jump aboard the second of the two remaining flatcars.

Courtesy Revelstoke Railway Museum c74932.

Edward's flatcar was pulled through an overnight blizzard by a steam locomotive like this one.

Through a bitter night of driving snow, Edward shivered along with the other men who were riding the rails. He felt shaken almost to pieces as the little train made its way slowly over the rough roadbed. No one was able to sleep. The snow turned to sleet, and Edward was thoroughly soaked by the time the train pulled onto a siding at Craigellachie. It was pitch dark, and Edward was stiff and half-frozen; he couldn't see where he was. It was all he could do to make out the shape of an empty boxcar on an adjoining track. He crawled inside and, exhausted, fell into a deep sleep.

CHAPTER 11

EDWARD AND THE LAST SPIKE

Edward tumbled from the boxcar cold, damp, and tired. He wiped the sleep from his eyes as his boots scrunched on the gravel where the boxcar had been shunted. He could just make out, through the bleak light of dawn, a shadowy gathering of men of various shapes and sizes. They were fitting the last steel rails into the final gap in the Canadian Pacific Railway. Edward drew his watch from his pocket and squinted to check the time: just after seven o'clock. He heaved a sigh of relief. There was still time to see the driving of the Last Spike!

Looking at the men, Edward saw several he recognized from his days in Farwell. He'd gotten to know a lot of them while riding the mail through Eagle Pass. He recognized some of the most important men connected with the railway. There was Major Albert Rogers, famous for discovering that pass through the Selkirk Mountains, which bore his name. He was directing the navvies as they hauled the final rails into place. His long white beard and his fancy vest and watch-chain gave him an air of importance. Colonel Sam Steele, one of the members of the original group of North-West Mounted Police that came West in 1874, stood guard over the lot. Colonel Steele looked like he was about to burst with pride, as if what was happening here today was all his doing.

"What's Major Rogers doing?" Edward asked one of the workers.

"Can't you see, kid? He's having us measure how to cut the last rails." As the man spoke, workers brought forward two rails which they laid beside the gap. Then they measured them for cutting: just over 7.77 metres. A foreman scored both rails to show where they should be cut. Edward winced as Major Rogers took up a huge bludgeon and began to pound first one, then the other, with a series of sharp blows. They both cracked just where they were supposed to and were quickly lifted into place. Major Rogers took it on himself to pound in the iron spikes to hold one rail in place. The second was left untouched for the ceremony.

With the driving of the Last Spike, the railway linked Canada coast-to-coast, and John A. Macdonald's promise to British Columbia was fulfilled.

Courtesy Revelstoke Railway Museum 03267.

Things were happening quickly now. Edward heard several sharp blasts of a steam whistle as the official train drew into sight a few hundred yards down the track. Slowing now, Locomotive 148 chugged to a stop. It had brought the ceremonial party to Craigellachie in comfort during a leisurely overnight trip from Farwell. The men had slept warm in their berths, while Edward and his companions clung to their bed of cold steel rails.

How Edward wished he had been on that train! *I'll bet they've just had a big breakfast*, he thought hungrily, as he watched the arrival. Steam escaped from the engine as if the great black monster was pausing to regain its breath. Everyone stood quietly and waited for the passengers to get off.

One after another, the distinguished men for whom this day had been arranged stepped from their parlour car. The photographer, Alexander Ross, was one of the first off the train. He was a stunted little man, with a crooked back. He walked all bent over, carrying his camera in a large black box. He held what looked like a tripod over his shoulder.

When it seemed as if everybody had dismounted, yet one more figure appeared on the step of the Matapedia. He was tall and exceedingly erect, with a tremendous white beard. On the top of his head he wore a large black top hat.

By now, Edward had worked his way around to a spot next to Mr. Ferguson.

American contractor Andrew Onderdonk brought thousands of Chinese labourers to build the Canadian Pacific Railway. He was given orders by Ottawa to cut costs, and hiring Chinese workers at low wages was the easiest way to do this.

The Man Who Drove the Spike

Donald A. Smith, the son of a Scottish tradesman, came to Canada to work as an apprentice clerk for the Hudson's Bay Company. He died rich and titled, as Lord Strathcona, remembered for having driven the Last Spike in the great railway in which he was an important investor. Forever after that day, he lived in the glory of his accomplishments for the CPR.

Smith worked his way up the ranks of the Hudson's Bay Company, eventually becoming its governor. He was as successful in politics as in business. While a member of parliament for the Selkirk District in Manitoba, he voted against John A. Macdonald's government for its involvement in the Pacific Scandal, which was caused by contributions Macdonald took from the railway's backers. Smith then became an investor, along with his cousin George Stephen, in a new company formed to finish the Canadian Pacific Railway.

Two years after driving the Last Spike, Smith became an MP again, this time for Montreal West, and was appointed president of the Bank of Montreal. In 1896 he was appointed Canada's high commissioner to Britain. He held that post, as well as that of governor of the Hudson's Bay Company, until his death in 1914.

In 1900, Lord Strathcona financed his own cavalry regiment of 500 men and horses, called Lord Strathcona's Horse, for the South African Boer War. He served as the chancellor of McGill University and founded Royal Victoria College for women in 1896.

"That's Mr. Smith, the man I told you about," he whispered to Edward. "They say he's a financial genius for having raised all that money."

No sooner had these men stretched their legs than Edward heard the echo of a whistle in the opposite direction. A train was coming in from the Pacific! It was pulling Andrew Onderdonk's private car, Eva, which came to a rest on the siding where the boxcar Edward had slept in still sat. It was Mr. Onderdonk's furious energy that had driven ten thousand workers to punch twin lines of steel through the mountains from Port Moody, at the head of Burrard Inlet, to Craigellachie.

Nothing stood between No. 148 and the Pacific Ocean, except one seven metre rail that needed only to be spiked to the wooden ties on which it rested.

The first man to greet Andrew Onderdonk was William Van Horne, the railway's general manager. He told Mr. Onderdonk that the CPR could never have been finished without him.

"You've done a marvellous job," Mr. Van Horne said before taking him over to say hello to Donald Smith and Mr. Ferguson. Edward thought Mr. Smith looked like Father Time himself, his great white beard falling down over his waistcoat, a stark contrast to the black stove pipe hat he was wearing. All the important men were gathering around them.

"We're all set for you to drive in the Last Spike," Mr. Rogers told the old patriarch of the CPR. Everybody crowded around the two of them, while Alexander Ross set up his tripod and camera a few feet down the track. He had one of the newer cameras of the time, which opened like an accordion and captured pictures on a plate of glass, storing it forever. Mr. Ross was wearing only a thin coat over his tweed suit and Edward saw him draw his hands to his mouth, breathing warmth onto his fingers.

Edward decided it was time to make his move. He pushed his way toward where Donald Smith held a large spike maul in his hands. The roadmaster, Frank Brothers, had tapped an iron spike into place.

"Can I get in?" Edward asked one of the men. He wanted to get as close as possible.

"Whadda yuh doin' here?" someone demanded. "Get away, kid!"

"Let him in, he can stand right there," a loud voice said. It was Mr. Ferguson.

"Don't you know that's the Craigellachie Kid?" he added.

Edward's heart was beating fast, and he forgot about his wet clothes and sodden boots. He straightened the black cap he was wearing, bent a bit to one side to avoid the flight of the hammer, propped his left foot on a tie, and held his breath.

Mr. Van Horne was standing directly behind Donald Smith, hands plunged into the pockets of his overcoat. He seemed to have a glum look on his face. A few steps from Mr. Van Horne, and right next to Edward, stood a mountain of a man, Sandford Fleming. He had a huge, flowing white beard and wore a big top hat. On the other side of the track, wearing his derby hat at a jaunty angle, was Mr. Van Horne's personal cook, Robert Pearson. Beside him was James Ross, the construction manager. Andrew Onderdonk and Colonel Steele were at the back of the crowd.

At exactly twenty-two minutes after nine o'clock, Donald Smith raised the heavy hammer over his head and brought it down on the spike with a crash. His aim was off and the spike lay there, half-in and badly bent. Frank Brothers, the roadmaster, quickly yanked it out and propped another in its place. Again, Donald Smith raised the big hammer over his head. This time it came down squarely on the spike. At the exact moment of the hammer's flight, the photographer pressed the shutter. More blows rained down on the spike and the camera snapped away. Everyone was silent as the Last Spike was driven home.

Courtesy McCord Museum, Montreal. *MP0000.25.971.*

Edward Mallandaine inserted himself into the picture when Alexander Ross took this Last Spike photo.

Even after Mr. Smith put the hammer aside, no one spoke for a moment. Edward sucked in his breath, amazed at what he had just seen. Then, as if on signal, a cheer broke out. It started with one man and spread through the crowd. Soon, train whistles were blown, adding to the noise.

"Speech, speech!" someone shouted.

But Mr. Smith remained silent. He looked at Mr. Van Horne, who turned to the crowd and said: "All I can say is that the work has been done well in every way."

Several more short speeches were made, and hands were shaken. No one seemed too excited, except for Mr. Rogers: there was a big smile on his face. He looked like he was unable to contain

Courtesy Revelstoke Railway Museum 03031.

The task of keeping trains running fell to a hardy band of locomotive engineers, like the men shown here.

himself. The old surveyor grabbed hold of a tie and upended it, then tried to stick it into the ground to mark the spot. Other men started picking up bits of rail and cast off spikes as souvenirs.

While the executives were congratulating themselves, workmen who had not been in any of the pictures approached the photographer.

"How about a picture of us?" one of them asked Mr. Ross. "We'd like something to remember this day."

They all walked back down the tracks a hundred yards before huddling together to have their picture taken. The shutter clicked time and again, taking more pictures that would find their way into future history books.

Then Locomotive 148 sounded its whistle.

"All aboard for the Pacific! Next stop, Port Moody."

The important men of the CPR returned to their parlour car to enjoy cigars and whisky. In a few minutes, the train began to move forward. It passed over the Last Spike and rolled along the twin rails of steel that would take it through green mountain passes and verdant river valleys, down to the blue Pacific and the new world of Canada's tomorrow.

When construction shut down along the railway, the Chinese labourers were the first to go. One night, weeks before the ceremony at Craigellachie, Dukesang Wong and his crew had been told they would no longer be needed. It was up to them to find their way out of Shuswap Valley, where they had been ballasting the railway.

Very few of the labourers had saved enough money to pay their way back to China, or for a comfortable life once they got there. Dukesong still dreamed of making a life for himself and his future wife, Lin, in Canada. He considered going to Victoria, where he knew there were many Chinese people, but he'd never been to that town. Dukesong had told Edward, he preferred to return to Saltwater City, where he had many friends and he was sure he would find a way to profitably occupy his time.

"Perhaps I will become a tailor. My countrymen must adapt to Western ways, and they will want Western clothing. I can learn to make it for them."

A few hours after the driving of the Last Spike, Edward scored a seat aboard a work train returning to Farwell. He went to the Columbia Hotel for one last night, where the talk in the lobby was about nothing other than the Last Spike. Edward was able to join right in, proudly telling everyone he met how he got himself in the photograph of the great event.

The next morning, he went to the shack that served as a temporary railway station to inquire about trains to Port Moody. There, he was told that there was no scheduled service, just work trains going back and forth. This meant Edward wouldn't have to pay for a ticket: he knew enough people to be able to hitch rides from place to place all the way back to the coast.

The trains to Port Moody stopped often to drop off supplies, and take on water and wood. It took Edward several days, and many train changes, to reach his destination. Along the way, he thought about everything he had seen and done. Of everything that had happened to him, nothing compared with being present for the Last Spike.

A Spike for History

The Last Spike remained in the tie where Donald Smith had driven it after the ceremony. The spike was probably discarded, though, at some point during routine replacement of the ties. The second-to-last bent spike that Smith had failed to drive in was given to him some time after the 1885 ceremony and his grandson presented it to Canada's National Museum of Science and Technology during a centennial ceremony at Craigellachie on November 7, 1985.

He was even prouder of the fact that he was in the picture of the great event. Edward wrote a letter to a friend describing every detail of his trip, and ended his letter with these words: "Thus, was the Dominion of Canada bound and nailed together by bands of steel."

Edward couldn't stop thinking about how things had turned out for him. He'd started out for the North-West Rebellion, but even though he was too late his trip wasn't for nothing. He'd made the most of it — maybe he'd even be in the history books. Who knew what would become of that picture?

CHAPTER 12

HOME FROM THE MOUNTAINS

The scent of the sea filled Edward's nostrils. He'd forgotten the tangy smell of salt air during his time in the mountains. His summer had been filled with the aroma of pine needles and alpine flowers. On the nights when he huddled in his bedroll, thrown under a tree on the forest floor at some convenient resting place on his rides between Farwell and Eagle Landing, their fragrance had been like perfume.

Edward stepped from the back platform of the caboose onto the rough wooden deck of the Port Moody station as the work train squealed to a stop. It had reached the tip of Burrard Inlet, the end of the line for the Canadian Pacific Railway. From the station, Edward could see a few boats tied up at the dock. He thanked the conductor for letting him share the comfort of his caboose.

"The next time you want to travel, you'll have to buy a ticket," the conductor told

Edward. "No more free rides once the passenger trains get rolling."

Edward considered going down to the dock to see what was happening, but he decided against it. He needed to travel a few miles overland to New Westminster, where he could catch a steamer that would take him home to Victoria.

His satchel under his arm, Edward strode off down the rutted road that served as Port Moody's main street. It had the usual collection of general stores, cafés, saloons, and ship provisioners. He asked the way to the stagecoach office, and was directed around a corner where he found a sign hanging over a false fronted building: PACIFIC STAGECOACH.

"Stage's leaving in five minutes," he was told. "Fare's a dollar and a half."

Edward paid willingly. He had saved up two hundred dollars from his summer riding parcels and the Royal Mail through Eagle Pass. He felt rich.

The first thing Edward did when the stagecoach arrived in New Westminster was to go to the Royal George hotel where he'd stayed on his way upcountry. The desk clerk recognized him.

Courtesy Revelstoke Railway Museum 01585.

The city of Revelstoke filled the horizon, as seen from Mt. Revelstoke around 1900.

"I remember you. You look different. Not as pale as I remember. You've grown up."

Edward was surprised by these remarks. He didn't think he was any different than on that summer day four months ago when he'd first asked for a room. Later, looking in the mirror he realized that he had changed. He detected the first signs of a beard and his hair was shaggy, hanging down over his collar. Edward straightened his shoulders and stuck out his chest. *I'm a man now, I know my way around.* It occurred to him that the haircut he'd been given by a camp cook back at Eagle Landing hadn't done much for him. He needed to improve his appearance; some new clothes might do it.

An hour later, Edward was back in his room with a bundle under his arm. There was a dry goods store across the street from the hotel, and he had bought new boots, a jacket, and a pair of strong, blue denim jeans brought up from San Francisco. The storekeeper told him they'd been made by some man named Levi Strauss. The whole lot cost him almost fifteen dollars.

I'll have to watch my money, Edward thought. *At this rate I'll soon be broke.*

Early the next morning, Edward waited at the docks on the Fraser River for the *Rainbow* to sail for Victoria. It got underway just after eight o'clock. He was excited at the thought of being home by evening. The time passed quickly. Edward struck up a conversation with a young man who was on his way to set up a law practice in Victoria. Edward amazed him with accounts of his experiences in the mountains. Afterward, he worried that he might have sounded boastful, but he couldn't stop himself from talking about his adventures — especially getting his picture taken at the Last Spike.

It was dark when the boat docked in Victoria. The Mallandaine house on Simcoe Street was but a short walk from where the *Rainbow* had tied up. Along the way, Edward picked up the scent of the city. There was an acrid smell of smoke, from the burning of sawdust at a mill, and the sweet aroma of roses that were still blooming in several yards. The streets were dark, except for one intersection that was lit by gaslight. There might have been a moon, but it was cloudy. It didn't matter to Edward; he was glad to be home.

The front door of his house opened quietly when Edward turned the knob. He stepped inside. He could make out the glow of a gas lamp in the parlour. "Hello?" he called out, "I'm home."

For a moment, there was no response. Then he heard the squeak of floorboards as someone came into the hallway. It was his father.

"Edward, I thought that sounded like you! You're back! Mother," he shouted. "Come directly. Edward's home."

Edward's father put one arm on his shoulder, shaking his hand vigorously. His mother was there in an instant. He fell into her arms.

"Let me look at you," she said. "Come into the parlour where I can see you. My, how you've grown. Hasn't he, Father? Where did you get those fine clothes?"

The joy of the reunion filled Edward with happiness.

"Where's the rest of the family?" His brother Charles suddenly tumbled down the stairs, followed by Frederick and the two girls, Louisa and Harriet. Charles danced around them while the others fired questions at Edward. Their chatter went on long into the night.

Edward had gifts for everyone. The most prized went to Charles: a rock into which the outline of a small sea creature was impressed. The railway workers had called it a "stone fish." It was a fossil Edward had picked up on the bank of the Columbia River. The fossil was evidence of the time when, eons ago, ocean waves lapped the shore of the continent and the great peaks of the Rockies had not yet been thrust up from the bottom of the sea.

Edward saved his greatest piece of news for the last, after he'd told his family all about meeting Judge Begbie and the governor general, and being robbed. Charles was nodding off when Edward finally told them about his presence at the driving of the Last Spike.

"I am in the picture," he said proudly. "The whole world will see I was there!"

Edward's first few days at home passed in a whirl. He was anxious to see his old school friends and tell them of what he'd been up to.

When Edward went to his friend Jimmy's house, he expected a warm welcome. Instead, his buddy treated him with coolness. He decided to tell him about being in the Last Spike picture. Before he could say anything, Jimmy told Edward that he'd heard about how he had had his picture taken. Jimmy didn't seem too pleased.

"Just because you've done all that," he told Edward, "doesn't make you any better than anybody else."

"I don't think I'm better than anyone," Edward said. But in his heart of hearts, Edward believed he'd done something that other boys of his age wouldn't have dared. Still, he didn't like his friend's resentment of his accomplishment, and no longer felt as brazenly sure of himself. Edward resolved not to boast about how he'd ridden the Royal Mail or had been present at the driving of the Last Spike any more. He kept the idea that someday, when the picture is published in school books, every kid in Canada will know about him to himself.

A week after Edward arrived home, the *British Colonist* reported the hanging of Louis Riel for treason. The paper said his execution, which took place in Regina, was cause for great indignation in Quebec. Bonfires were lit in the streets of Montreal and riots broke out in several places. There were other hangings, but none created the ill-feeling that arose between the French and English than the fate of the instigator of the North-West Rebellion.

Edward gave little thought to all this. He was more concerned about his father's reminder of his promise to return to his architecture apprenticeship. His mother also chimed in, questioning him about his plans for the future. It seemed he wasn't to be given any time to decide what to do.

"Why must I make up my mind right now?" Edward wondered aloud.

The excitement of Craigellachie had barely worn off and here he was, being forced to choose what to do next. Architecture didn't sound so exciting anymore.

Edward's father made up his mind for him: "You'll come back to the office, or you can't stay here."

Edward thought about leaving home again, but decided that he needed more time to make up his mind. Going back to his father's office would give him time to think things over, at least.

Edward resolved to learn all he could about architecture. His father's assistant began to teach him the principles of design and set him to work at a drafting table, where he learned to sketch floor plans and indicate the locations of doors and windows. As the months went by, Edward became comfortable working at the table in the corner of his father's office. He got to accompany his father to sites where new houses were being built. And before long he began to create some of his own architectural plans from scratch.

Edward's mother was glad to have her son home, but she worried about what would become of him. She noticed that he was getting interested in girls. "We must take care to see he meets the proper type," she told Edward Sr. Louisa Mallandaine still held to the sensibilities of the Victorian society in which she'd grown up in England. She believed that people must marry within their own class and respect those further up the social ladder.

"Don't worry about Edward," her husband told her. "He'll make his own way. This is a new country, you know. That old stuff went on in England, but it doesn't count for much here."

Some of Louisa's concerns must have rubbed off on Edward. At times, he felt desperate about his life and what might become of him. He wanted to know himself better. When he heard about the phrenologist on Fort Street, he decided he must visit her. He'd heard many people speak in favour of phrenology, even if they didn't understand it. You could read a person's character by the bumps on their heads; the shape of a person's skull had something to do with what's in their brain.

Mrs. Thornton, the phrenologist, was a heavy-set woman clad in a long black dress. She held a lorgnette — a pair of glasses fixed to a fancy handle — and told Edward that her fee to read his head was twenty-five cents. Edward handed over the coin and sat in a chair in front of her. She stood behind him, and Edward could feel her running her fingers over the top of his skull, probing for bumps and fissures.

The examination took only a few minutes. Mrs. Thornton retired to a back room, and when she emerged, she handed Edward a card on which she'd rated the qualities of his character. There was a scale of one to seven. Edward wasn't surprised when he saw he'd been given a rating of seven for appetite. He was rated six for mirth and wit, and five and a half for sexual love. Edward didn't know anything about sexual love, but he felt reassured that he'd done so well in that department. But when he saw that he'd gotten just a two for respect for others, he swore he would do better in the future.

At home, Edward noticed a difference in his father and mother. They seemed to be older and quieter than he had remembered them. Edward Sr. spent hours painting pictures of Victoria and scenes of the countryside; Louisa spent her time in her favourite rocking chair, sewing. His brothers and sisters, too, seemed to be more grown up. Charles didn't want to roughhouse as much as he used to and Frederick started keeping to himself. His sisters … well, they were just girls.

Edward didn't entirely realize it, but his life was unfolding before him. The rest of the world was changing, too. The first regular through train from Montreal reached Port Moody the summer after Edward arrived home, on July 4, 1886. It took just five days and nineteen hours. Before the railway, a journey across Canada took anywhere from eight to twelve weeks.

The first train to reach Port Moody. The railway had cut the travel time from Montreal from five weeks to five days and seventeen hours. The railway terminus was later moved to Vancouver.

Edward was surprised, along with everybody else, when he heard that the CPR had decided to extend the railway to a place known as Granville, or Gastown, since some people called the village after Gassy Jack, a pioneer saloon keeper. Mr. Stephen thought it needed a more respectable name and decided to call it Vancouver in honour of Captain George Vancouver, the British naval officer who had first sailed around the island that would bear his name. Besides, the name was well known in England, and it would be good for business to name the city after such an illustrious figure. Not long after, the whole place burned to the ground. But just as had happened in Farwell, it was rebuilt faster and bigger than ever before.

By now, Edward was beginning to find life at home dull, even stifling. He longed for the freedom he'd enjoyed watching the railway construction and riding the Royal Mail.

He was a man now, and he knew he couldn't rely on his father for a job forever. He decided that he must return to the mountains. It was there he would feel at home again.

Courtesy Revelstoke Railway Museum 01245.

Trains were sometimes derailed by landslides and wash-outs, as shown in this photograph of the wreckage of a steam engine.

Edward thought of the mountains of British Columbia as monuments to the dawn of history. He wasn't sure what great force had brought them about, or when. He only knew that when the sun shone on their savage peaks, and cast dark shadows into their deep chasms, there was no sight like it. He'd seen black bears feast on berries in summer and fish salmon from the Eagle River in fall. He'd watched mule dear and mountain goats browse on the last greenery of the season. He had heard that mountain lions prowled the forests of lodgepole pine, though he had never seen any. He'd seen wild flowers bloom in gold and amethyst, preparing for their return to the thin soil come winter.

He also understood that the passage of the railway through the mountains had forever changed life on and around them. He'd been there when the sound of change was first heard; the mysterious whistle of escaping steam that signalled the presence of man. It had echoed against the peaks throughout the night and at dawn on November 7, 1885, when the train that he rode into Craigellachie squealed to a halt. He was there for the act of Canadian nation building that took place on that historic day. He knew now that one day he would have to return to the mountains. Their call was irresistible.

The Trains Still Run

The Canadian Pacific Railway may have abandoned passenger service and has closed many of its lines, but its freight trains still run from Montreal to Vancouver and major American cities, such as Chicago and New York.

Today, many people want a new era of railway construction that would give Canadians high speed trains between such points as Windsor and Quebec City, and Calgary and Edmonton.

Canada today is a vastly different nation than the one that was bound together by the Last Spike. The Internet, cellphones, and iPods provide instant communication and entertainment. Canadians celebrate their multicultural diversity and respect the First Nations people. But the memory of that long ago occasion, when Edward Mallandaine watched Donald Smith swing the hammer that changed Canadian history, will never fade away. The click of the photographer's shutter that stilled the morning's mist has seen to that.

EPILOGUE

Edward Mallandaine never forgot his moment as the Boy in the Picture.

In 1889, at the age of twenty-two, Edward left what he considered a dull life in Victoria to strike out for the Kootenay region, then virgin territory in the remote southeastern corner of the province. He was hired by the man who had built the Panama Canal to lay out a new railway from the United States into British Columbia. That experience qualified him as both a civil engineer and a forester.

Edward and his lifelong friend Fred Little became business partners and the two of them staked a 180-acre site for the future town of Creston. It had a perfect setting on the shoulder of Goat Mountain overlooking the fields below Kootenay Lake. In a deal to gain the town a CPR station, they gave the railway half the townsite and Edward became the land agent. He had control over several million acres and, in 1911, scoured Europe for immigrants willing to come to British Columbia.

Edward showed great foresight in everything he did. The valleys of the Kootenay region had great potential for agriculture, but without water nothing could be grown. He worked with various promoters to build dykes and canals to divert water from the region's rivers onto the flat lands in its valleys. His first project irrigated thousands of acres in the Windermere Valley. He was also an enthusiastic supporter of the successful scheme to dyke the Creston Flats.

Edward went to France during the First World War as the major in charge of the Kootenay Regiment of the Canadian Overseas Forestry Corps. He later became a colonel in the Canadian Army Reserve, a title he was known by the rest of his life. Colonel Mallandaine

was the whole show in Creston — reeve (mayor), head of the school board, the hospital, the board of trade, and owner of the town's waterworks.

Edward married Creston's first school teacher, Jean Ramsay. They had no children, but he loved to tell the town's school children how he became the Boy in the Picture. He returned to Revelstoke in 1945 for the sixtieth anniversary celebration of the Last Spike. Edward died in 1949 at the age of eighty-two.

Edward Mallandaine attends the sixtieth anniversary celebration of the Last Spike in Revelstoke in 1945. Young Lewis Davis of Revelstoke played Edward in a reenactment of the ceremony.

Courtesy Revelstoke Museum 1563.

BIBLIOGRAPHY

PRIMARY

British Columbia Archives, Edward Mallandaine, MS-1214, MS-2565; Edward Mallandaine Sr., MS-0470.

Library and Archives Canada, Edward Mallandaine, File RG150, Box 5869-53.

NEWSPAPERS AND MAGAZINES

Allison, Sidney. "The Boy in the Photo." *The Islander,* May 29, 2005.

Argyle, Ray. "The Boy in the Picture." *The Beaver*, August–September 2008.

British Colonist. Accounts of the North-West Rebellion, various dates, 1885.

"Eager Youth in Famous Picture Identified After Fifty Years." *Canadian Pacific Staff Bulletin*, February 1939.

"Founder of Creston, Col. Mallandaine Dies." *The Review*, August 4, 1949.

"A Great Citizen, a Great Canadian." *The Review*, August 11, 1949.

Laux, Bill. "A Kootenay Saga." *British Columbia History*, Vol. 41, No. 4.

Mallandaine, E. "Reminiscing." *The Review*, 1939–1945.

McKelvie, B.A. "He Set Victoria's Harbour on Fire." *Vancouver Province*, February 17, 1929.

BOOKS

Andrew, Robert. *We Are Their Children*. Vancouver, B.C.: CommCept Publishing, 1977.

Berton, Pierre. *The Last Spike: The Great Railway 1881–1885*. Toronto: Doubleday Canada, 1971.

Cottingham, Mollie E. *Kootenay Chronicles*. Vancouver: University of British Columbia, 1947.

BIBLIOGRAPHY

Daem M., and Dickey, E.E. *A History of Early Revelstoke.* Revelstoke, B.C.: Privately published, 1962.

Davies, Colin. *Louis Riel and the New Nation.* Toronto: Book Society of Canada, 1980.

Koopman, Carol. *Louis Riel.* Calgary: Weigl Educational Publishers, 2008.

Liu, Julia Ningyu. *Canadian Steel Chinese Grit: A Tribute to the Chinese Who Worked on Canada's Railroads.* Vancouver, B.C.: Paxlink Communications Inc., 2000.

Nobbs, Ruby. *Rail Tales from the Revelstoke Division.* Altona, M.B.: Friesens Corp., 2000.

Turner, Robert D. *West of the Great Divide.* Winlaw, B.C.: Sononis Press, 1987.

Watters, Reginald Eyre. *British Columbia.* Toronto: McClelland and Stewart Ltd., 1957.

Wolf, Adolf & Okan Hungry, *Canadian Railway Stories: 100 Years of History and Lore.* Skookumchuck, B.C.: Good Medicine Books, 1985.

WEB SITES

"Building the Canadian Pacific Railway"
www.collectionscanada.gc.ca/settlement/kids/021013-2031.3-e.html

"Chinese Immigration to Canada"
archives.cbc.ca/society/racism/topics/1433-9242

"Chinese and the CPR"
www.city.kamloops.bc.ca/museum/archives/pdfs/N308%20-%20The%20Chinese%20and%20
the%20CPR.pdf

"Mallandaine Family"
members.shaw.ca/mallandaine

"Story of the Canadian Pacific Railway"
www8.cpr.ca/cms/nr/cprinternet/images/cprchildrenshistory.pdf

INDEX

ABOUT THE AUTHOR

Ray Argyle grew up in the British Columbia mountain community of Creston, the town that Edward Mallandaine helped found after having been present for the driving of the Last Spike of the Canadian Pacific Railway. Ray's early memories are of fishing in the rivers, swimming in the lakes, and climbing the mountains that rose up behind his home.

These pastimes always left him time for reading, and Ray decided early on to be a writer. He got his first newspaper job fresh out of school and later worked for the global news agency British United Press, as a correspondent and bureau manager. This included a stint covering the British Columbia Legislature in Victoria, where he often strolled past Edward Mallandaine's boyhood home. Ray later worked for the old *Toronto Telegram* where he was editor of the Telegram News Service.

Ray established Argyle Communications Inc., a corporate communications company, and has worked with business and government leaders around the world. He has been a school trustee, and a trustee of the McMichael Canadian Art Collection in Kleinburg, Ontario.

Besides *The Boy in the Picture* his books include *Turning Points: the Campaigns that Changed Canada* and *Scott Joplin and the Age of Ragtime*. He has written for *Reader's Digest*, *Canada's History Magazine* (formerly *The Beaver*), the *National Post* and other publications.

Ray has three daughters and four grandchildren. He and his partner Deborah Windsor divide their time between Toronto and Kingston, Ontario.

MORE GREAT NON-FICTION FOR YOUNG PEOPLE

Sergeant Gander
A Canadian Hero
by Robyn Walker
978-1-55488-463-6
$19.99

Sergeant Gander is a fascinating account of the Royal Rifles of Canada's canine mascot, and his devotion to duty demonstrated during the Battle of Hong Kong in the Second World War. Armed only with his formidable size, an intimidating set of teeth, and a protective instinct, Gander fought alongside his fellow Canadian soldiers. For his service in battle, Sergeant Gander was awarded the Dickin Medal, the animal equivalent to the Victoria Cross for humans. This honour is dedicated to animals displaying gallantry and devotion to duty while under any control of the armed forces. Sergeant Gander is the nineteenth dog to receive this medal and the first Canadian canine to do so.

The Underground Railroad
Next Stop, Toronto!
by Adrienne Shadd
978-1-55488-429-2
$16.99

The Underground Railroad: Next Stop, Toronto! stands out as an engaging and highly readable account of the lives of Black people in Toronto in the 1800s. This a richly illustrated book examines the urban connection of the clandestine system of secret routes, safe houses, and "conductors." Not only does it trace the story of the Underground Railroad itself and how people courageously made the trip north to Canada and freedom, but it also explores what happened to them after they arrived. And it does so using never-before-published information on the African-Canadian community of Toronto. Based entirely on new research carried out for the experiential theatre show "The Underground Railroad: Next Stop, Freedom!" at the Royal Ontario Museum, this volume offers new insights into the rich heritage of the Black people who made Toronto their home before the Civil War. It portrays life in the city during the nineteenth century in considerable detail.

The Real Winnie
A One-of-a-Kind Bear
by Val Shushkewich
978-1-89621-989-9
$16.95

The story of Winnie, the real Canadian bear that captured the heart of Christopher, son of A.A. Milne, and became immortalized in the Winnie the Pooh stories, is told against the backdrop of the First World War. In August 1914, a Canadian soldier and veterinarian named Lieutenant Harry Colebourn, en route to a training camp in Quebec, purchased a black bear cub in White River, Ontario, which he named Winnipeg.

First a regimental mascot for Canadians training for wartime service, Winnie then became a star attraction at the London Zoo, and ultimately inspired one of the best-loved characters in children's literature. For those many generations of readers who adored Winnie the Pooh, and for those intrigued by the unique stories embedded in Canadian history, this book is a feast of information about a one-of-a-kind bear set during a poignant period of world history.

Available at your favourite bookseller.

DUNDURN PRESS
www.dundurn.com

What did you think of this book? Visit www.dundurn.com for reviews, videos, updates, and more!

Marquis Book Printing Inc.

Québec, Canada
2010